Excel 2010: Basic

Instructor's Edition

Excel 2010: Basic

President, Axzo Press:	Jon Winder
Vice President, Product Development:	Charles G. Blum
Vice President, Operations:	Josh Pincus
Director of Publishing Systems Development:	Dan Quackenbush
Developmental Editor:	Laurie Perry
Copyeditor:	Catherine Oliver
Keytester:	Cliff Coryea

Trademarks

Disclaimer

ISBN 10: 1-4260-2154-2
ISBN 13: 978-1-4260-2154-1

Printed in the United States of America

5 6 7 8 9 10 11 GL 16 15 14 13 12

What is the Microsoft ® Office Specialist Program?

The Microsoft Office Specialist Program enables candidates to show that they have something exceptional to offer – proven expertise in certain Microsoft programs. Recognized by businesses and schools around the world, over 4 million certifications have been obtained in over 100 different countries. The Microsoft Office Specialist Program is the only Microsoft-approved certification program of its kind.

What is the Microsoft Office Specialist Certification?

The Microsoft Office Specialist certification validates through the use of exams that you have obtained specific skill sets within the applicable Microsoft Office programs and other Microsoft programs included in the Microsoft Office Specialist Program. The candidate can choose which exam(s) they want to take according to which skills they want to validate.

The available Microsoft Office Specialist Program exams include*:
- Using Windows Vista®
- Using Microsoft® Office Word 2007
- Using Microsoft® Office Word 2007 - Expert
- Using Microsoft® Office Excel® 2007
- Using Microsoft® Office Excel® 2007 - Expert
- Using Microsoft® Office PowerPoint® 2007
- Using Microsoft® Office Access® 2007
- Using Microsoft® Office Outlook® 2007
- Using Microsoft SharePoint® 2007

The Microsoft Office Specialist Program 2010 exams will include*:
- Microsoft Word 2010
- Microsoft Word 2010 Expert
- Microsoft Excel® 2010
- Microsoft Excel® 2010 Expert
- Microsoft PowerPoint® 2010
- Microsoft Access® 2010
- Microsoft Outlook® 2010
- Microsoft SharePoint® 2010

What does the Microsoft Office Specialist Approved Courseware logo represent?

The logo indicates that this courseware has been approved by Microsoft to cover the course objectives that will be included in the relevant exam. It also means that after utilizing this courseware, you may be better prepared to pass the exams required to become a certified Microsoft Office Specialist.

For more information:

To learn more about Microsoft Office Specialist exams, visit www.microsoft.com/learning/msbc

To learn about other Microsoft approved courseware from Axzo Press, visit http://www.axzopress.com.

Contents

Introduction

After reading this introduction, you will know how to:

A Use ILT Series manuals in general.

B Use prerequisites, a target student description, course objectives, and a skills inventory to properly set students' expectations for the course.

C Set up a classroom to teach this course.

D Get support for setting up and teaching this course.

Topic A: About the manual

ILT Series philosophy

Our goal is to make you, the instructor, as successful as possible. To that end, our manuals facilitate students' learning by providing structured interaction with the software itself. While we provide text to help you explain difficult concepts, the hands-on activities are the focus of our courses. Leading the students through these activities will teach the skills and concepts effectively.

We believe strongly in the instructor-led class. For many students, having a thinking, feeling instructor in front of them will always be the most comfortable way to learn. Because the students' focus should be on you, our manuals are designed and written to facilitate your interaction with the students, and not to call attention to manuals themselves.

We believe in the basic approach of setting expectations, then teaching, and providing summary and review afterwards. For this reason, lessons begin with objectives and end with summaries. We also provide overall course objectives and a course summary to provide both an introduction to and closure on the entire course.

Our goal is your success. We encourage your feedback in helping us to continually improve our manuals to meet your needs.

Manual components

The manuals contain these major components:

- Table of contents
- Introduction
- Units
- Course summary
- Glossary
- Index

Each element is described below.

Table of contents

The table of contents acts as a learning roadmap for you and the students.

Introduction

The introduction contains information about our training philosophy and our manual components, features, and conventions. It contains target student, prerequisite, objective, and setup information for the specific course. Finally, the introduction contains support information.

Units

Units are the largest structural component of the actual course content. A unit begins with a title page that lists objectives for each major subdivision, or topic, within the unit. Within each topic, conceptual and explanatory information alternates with hands-on activities. Units conclude with a summary comprising one paragraph for each topic, and an independent practice activity that gives students an opportunity to practice the skills they've learned.

The conceptual information takes the form of text paragraphs, exhibits, lists, and tables. The activities are structured in two columns, one telling students what to do, the other providing explanations, descriptions, and graphics. Throughout a unit, instructor notes are found in the left margin.

Course summary

This section provides a text summary of the entire course. It is useful for providing closure at the end of the course. The course summary also indicates the next course in this series, if there is one, and lists additional resources students might find useful as they continue to learn about the software.

Glossary

The glossary provides definitions for all of the key terms used in this course.

Index

The index at the end of this manual makes it easy for you and your students to find information about a particular software component, feature, or concept.

Manual conventions

We've tried to keep the number of elements and the types of formatting to a minimum in the manuals. We think this aids in clarity and makes the manuals more classically elegant looking. But there are some conventions and icons you should know about.

Instructor note/icon

Item	Description
Italic text	In conceptual text, indicates a new term or feature.
Bold text	In unit summaries, indicates a key term or concept. In an independent practice activity, indicates an explicit item that you select, choose, or type.
`Code font`	Indicates code or syntax.
`Longer strings of ▶ code will look ▶ like this.`	In the hands-on activities, any code that's too long to fit on a single line is divided into segments by one or more continuation characters (▶). This code should be entered as a continuous string of text.
	In the left margin, provide tips, hints, and warnings for the instructor.
Select **bold item**	In the left column of hands-on activities, bold sans-serif text indicates an explicit item that you select, choose, or type.
Keycaps like (↵ ENTER)	Indicate a key on the keyboard you must press.
	Warnings prepare instructors for potential classroom management problems.
	Tips give extra information the instructor can share with students.
	Setup notes provide a realistic business context for instructors to share with students, or indicate additional setup steps required for the current activity.
	Projector notes indicate that there is a PowerPoint slide for the adjacent content.

Instructor notes.

⚠ *Warning icon.*

TIPS✔ *Tip icon.*

▱ *Setup icon.*

▱ *Projector icon.*

Hands-on activities

The hands-on activities are the most important parts of our manuals. They are divided into two primary columns. The "Here's how" column gives short directions to the students. The "Here's why" column provides explanations, graphics, and clarifications. To the left, instructor notes provide tips, warnings, setups, and other information for the instructor only. Here's a sample:

Do it!

A-1:   Creating a commission formula

Take the time to make sure your students understand this worksheet. We'll be here a while.

Here's how	Here's why
1 Open Sales	This is an oversimplified sales compensation worksheet. It shows sales totals, commissions, and incentives for five sales reps.
2 Observe the contents of cell F4	F4 ▼ = =E4*C_Rate
	The commission rate formulas use the name "C_Rate" instead of a value for the commission rate.

For these activities, we have provided a collection of data files designed to help students learn each skill in a real-world business context. As students work through the activities, they will modify and update these files. Of course, students might make a mistake and therefore want to re-key the activity starting from scratch. To make it easy to start over, students will rename each data file at the end of the first activity in which the file is modified. Our convention for renaming files is to add the word "My" to the beginning of the file name. In the above activity, for example, students are using a file called "Sales" for the first time. At the end of this activity, they would save the file as "My sales," thus leaving the "Sales" file unchanged. If students make mistakes, they can start over using the original "Sales" file.

In some activities, however, it might not be practical to rename the data file. Such exceptions are indicated with an instructor note. If students want to retry one of these activities, you will need to provide a fresh copy of the original data file.

PowerPoint presentations

Each unit in this course has an accompanying PowerPoint presentation. These slide shows are designed to support your classroom instruction while providing students with a visual focus. Each presentation begins with a list of unit objectives and ends with a unit summary slide. We strongly recommend that you run these presentations from the instructor's station as you teach this course. A copy of PowerPoint Viewer is included, so it is not necessary to have PowerPoint installed on your computer.

The ILT Series PowerPoint add-in

The CD also contains a PowerPoint add-in that enables you to do two things:

- Create slide notes for the class
- Display a control panel for the Flash movies embedded in the presentations

To load the PowerPoint add-in:

1 Copy the Course_ILT.ppa file to a convenient location on your hard drive.

2 Start PowerPoint.

3 Choose Tools, Macro, Security to open the Security dialog box. On the Security Level tab, select Medium (if necessary), and then click OK.

4 Choose Tools, Add-Ins to open the Add-Ins dialog box. Then, click Add New.

5 Browse to and double-click the Course_ILT.ppa file, and then click OK. A message box will appear, warning you that macros can contain viruses.

6 Click Enable Macros. The Course_ILT add-in should now appear in the Available Add-Ins list (in the Add-Ins dialog box). The "x" in front of Course_ILT indicates that the add-in is loaded.

7 Click Close to close the Add-Ins dialog box.

After you complete this procedure, a new toolbar will be available at the top of the PowerPoint window. This toolbar contains a single button labeled "Create SlideNotes." Click this button to generate slide-notes files in both text (.txt) and Excel (.xls) format. By default, these files will be saved to the folder that contains the presentation. If the PowerPoint file is on a CD-ROM or in some other location to which the slide-notes files cannot be saved, you will be prompted to save the presentation to your hard drive and try again.

When you run a presentation and come to a slide that contains a Flash movie, you will see a small control panel in the lower-left corner of the screen. You can use this panel to start, stop, and rewind the movie, or to play it again.

Topic B: Setting student expectations

Properly setting students' expectations is essential to your success. This topic will help you do that by providing:

- Prerequisites for this course
- A description of the target student
- A list of the objectives for the course
- A skills assessment for the course

Course prerequisites

Students taking this course should be familiar with personal computers and the use of a keyboard and a mouse. Furthermore, this course assumes that students have completed the following course or have equivalent experience:

- *Windows XP: Basic, Windows Vista: Basic,* or *Windows 7: Basic*

Target student

Students taking this course should be comfortable using a personal computer and Microsoft Windows XP, Windows Vista, or preferably Windows 7. They should have little or no experience using Microsoft Excel or any other spreadsheet program. Students will get the most out of this course if their goal is to become proficient in using Microsoft Excel to create basic worksheets and charts for data tracking and reporting.

Course objectives

You should share these overall course objectives with your students at the beginning of the day. This will give the students an idea about what to expect, and it will help you identify students who might be misplaced. Students are considered misplaced when they lack the prerequisite knowledge or when they already know most of the subject matter to be covered.

Note: In addition to the general objectives listed below, specific Microsoft Office Specialist exam objectives are listed at the beginning of each topic (where applicable) and are highlighted by instructor notes.

After completing this course, students will know how to:

- Start Microsoft Excel and identify the components of the Excel interface; open an Excel workbook; use the Help window; and navigate worksheets.

- Enter and edit text, values, and formulas; examine the order of operations; insert pictures; use AutoFill; save and update a workbook; and save a workbook as a PDF file.

- Move and copy data and formulas; use the Office Clipboard; use Paste Link; work with relative and absolute references; and insert and delete ranges, rows, and columns.

- Use the SUM function, AutoSum, and the AVERAGE, MIN, MAX, COUNT, and COUNTA functions to perform calculations in a worksheet.

- Format cells, rows, and columns; merge cells; apply color and borders; format numbers; create conditional formats; copy formatting; apply table styles; sort data; and use Find and Replace to update the formatting for specific content.

- Check spelling; find and replace text and data; preview and print a worksheet; set page orientation and margins; create and format headers and footers; and print gridlines.

- Create, format, modify, and print charts based on worksheet data; work with various chart elements; and apply chart types and chart styles.

- Freeze panes and split a worksheet; open and arrange a new window with the current worksheet content; hide and unhide data; set print titles and page breaks to optimize print output; insert different even and odd headers; and manage multiple worksheets.

- Represent data graphically within cells by applying three forms of conditional formatting (data bars, color scales, and icon sets); insert and modify SmartArt graphics; and insert and modify screenshots.

Skills inventory

Use the following form to gauge students' skill levels entering the class (students have copies in the introductions of their student manuals). For each skill listed, have students rate their familiarity from 1 to 5, with five being the most familiar. Emphasize that this is not a test. Rather, it is intended to provide students with an idea of where they're starting from at the beginning of class. If a student is wholly unfamiliar with all the skills, he or she might not be ready for the class. A student who seems to understand all of the skills, on the other hand, might need to move on to the next course in the series.

Skill	1	2	3	4	5
Starting Microsoft Excel					
Identifying Excel interface components					
Identifying worksheet components					
Using Help					
Navigating in a worksheet					
Opening and closing workbooks					
Saving workbooks					
Entering and editing text and values					
Using AutoFill to complete a series					
Entering formulas					
Inserting, moving, and resizing pictures					
Saving a workbook as a PDF file					
Moving and copying data and formulas					
Applying absolute references					
Inserting and deleting ranges					
Using the SUM, AVERAGE, MIN, MAX, COUNT, and COUNTA functions					
Using the AutoSum button					
Formatting text and numbers					
Adjusting column width and row height					
Aligning content					
Applying color to rows, columns, and individual cells					

Skill	1	2	3	4	5
Applying cell borders					
Applying conditional formatting					
Copying formatting					
Applying cell styles and table styles					
Checking spelling in worksheets					
Using Find and Replace to change text and values					
Previewing and printing one or more worksheets					
Changing page orientation					
Setting margins					
Creating and formatting headers and footers					
Creating charts based on worksheet data					
Applying chart types and chart styles					
Formatting chart elements					
Creating and editing a pie chart					
Freezing panes and splitting worksheets					
Hiding and unhiding data					
Setting print titles and page breaks					
Renaming, inserting, copying, moving, and deleting worksheets					
Using data bars, color scales, and icon sets as conditional formatting					
Inserting and modifying SmartArt graphics					
Inserting and modifying screenshots					

Topic C: Classroom setup

All our courses assume that each student has a personal computer to use during the class. Our hands-on approach to learning requires that they do. This topic gives information on how to set up the classroom to teach this course.

Hardware requirements

Each student's personal computer should have:

- A keyboard and a mouse
- 1 GHz processor (or faster)
- 1 GB RAM (or higher)
- 2 GB of available hard disk space after operating system install
- CD or DVD drive
- SVGA monitor at 1024 × 768 or higher resolution

Software requirements

You will need the following software:

- Microsoft Windows 7
- Microsoft Office 2010 (minimally, you can install only Excel)
- Adobe Reader
- A printer driver (An actual printer is not required, but students will not be able to complete Activity A-3 in the "Printing" unit or Activity B-1 in the "Managing large workbooks" unit unless a printer driver is installed.)

Network requirements

The following network components and connectivity are also required for this course:

- Internet access, for the following purposes:
  - Updating the Windows operating system and Microsoft Office 2010
  - Opening Help files at Microsoft Office Online
    (If online Help is not available, students will not be able to complete Activity C-1 in the unit titled "Getting started.")
  - Navigating to a Web page in Internet Explorer
    (If an Internet connection is not available, students will not be able to complete Activity C-1 in the unit titled "Graphics and screenshots.")
  - Downloading the Student Data files from www.axzopress.com
    (if necessary)

Classroom setup instructions

Before you teach this course, you will need to perform the following steps to set up each student computer.

1   Install Windows 7 on an NTFS partition according to the software publisher's instructions. After installation is complete, if the student machines have Internet access, use Windows Update to install any critical updates and Service Packs.

Note: You can also use Windows Vista or Windows XP, but the screenshots in this course were taken in Windows 7, so students' screens will look different.

2   With flat-panel displays, we recommend using the panel's native resolution for best results. Color depth/quality should be set to High (24 bit) or higher.

3   Install Microsoft Office 2010 according to the software manufacturer's instructions, as follows:

  a   When prompted for the CD key, enter the code included with your software and click Continue.

  b   On the next screen, click Customize.

  c   Click the Installation Options tab.

  d   For Microsoft Office Excel, Office Shared Features, and Office Tools, click the down-arrow and choose "Run all from My Computer."

  e   Set all *except* the following to Not Available: Microsoft Office Excel, Office Shared Features, and Office Tools.

  f   Click Install Now.

  g   On the last screen of the Office 2010 installer, click Continue Online. Internet Explorer displays the Office Online Web site, and the installer window closes.

  h   On the Office Online Web page, click the Downloads tab. Download and install any available updates.

  i   Close Internet Explorer.

4   Install Adobe Reader.

  a   In your browser, go to http://get.adobe.com/reader/.

  b   Click Download.

  c   If a notification appears at the top of the browser window, click it and choose Run Add-on.

5   If you have the data disc that came with this manual, locate the Student Data folder on it and copy it to the desktop of each student computer.

If you don't have the data disc, you can download the Student Data files for the course:

  a   Connect to www.axzopress.com.

  b   Under Downloads, click Instructor-Led Training.

  c   Browse the subject categories to locate your course. Then click the course title to display a list of available downloads. (You can also access these downloads through our Catalog listings.)

  d   Click the link(s) for downloading the Student Data files. You can download the files directly to student machines or to a central location on your own network.

  e   Create a folder named Student Data on the desktop of each student computer.

  f Double-click the downloaded zip file(s) and drag the contents into the Student Data folder.

6 Start Microsoft Office Excel 2010. Then do the following:

  a Activate the software. After activation, the Welcome to the 2010 Microsoft Office System dialog box appears.

  b Select "Don't make changes" and click Finish.

7 Disable Protected View settings for Excel as follows:

  a On the File tab, click Options.

  b Select Trust Center and click Trust Center Settings.

  c Select Protected View and clear "Enable Protected View for files originating from the Internet."

  d Click OK twice to save the settings. Close Excel.

CertBlaster software

CertBlaster pre- and post-assessment software is available for this course. To download and install this free software, students should complete the following steps:

1 Go to www.axzopress.com.

2 Under Downloads, click CertBlaster.

3 Click the link for Excel 2010.

4 Save the .EXE file to a folder on your hard drive. (**Note:** If you skip this step, the CertBlaster software will not install correctly.)

5 Click Start and choose Run.

6 Click Browse and navigate to the folder that contains the .EXE file.

7 Select the .EXE file and click Open.

8 Click OK and follow the on-screen instructions. When prompted for the password, enter **c_xl2010**.

Topic D: Support

Your success is our primary concern. If you need help setting up this class or teaching a particular unit, topic, or activity, please don't hesitate to get in touch with us.

Contacting us

Please contact us through our Web site, www.axzopress.com. You will need to provide the name of the course, and be as specific as possible about the kind of help you need.

Instructor's tools

Our Web site provides several instructor's tools for each course, including course outlines and answers to frequently asked questions. To download these files, go to www.axzopress.com. Then, under Downloads, click Instructor-Led Training and browse our subject categories.

Unit 1
Getting started

Unit time: 30 minutes

Complete this unit, and you'll know how to:

A Define a spreadsheet and identify spreadsheet components.

B Identify the main components of the Excel window.

C Use the Help window.

D Open and navigate workbooks.

Topic A: Spreadsheet terminology

Explanation

Excel is an electronic spreadsheet program that is part of the Microsoft Office suite. You use Excel to organize, calculate, and analyze data. The tasks you can perform range from preparing a simple invoice to creating elaborate 3-D charts to managing an accounting ledger for a company.

In Excel, you work with *worksheets*, which consist of rows and columns that intersect to form *cells*. Cells contain various kinds of data that you can format, sort, and analyze. An Excel file is called a *workbook*, which by default contains three blank worksheets.

Components of a spreadsheet

All spreadsheets, whether on ledger paper or in an electronic spreadsheet program, have common elements. Exhibit 1-1 shows some of these common elements.

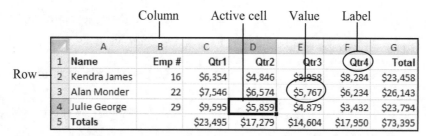

Exhibit 1-1: Spreadsheet components

The following table describes common spreadsheet elements.

Item	Description
Row	A horizontal group of cells in a worksheet. There are more than a million rows in an Excel worksheet. Each row is identified by a row number.
Column	A vertical group of cells in a worksheet. Each column is identified by one or more letters. The 26th column is column Z. The 27th is AA. When all of the double letters are used up, through ZZ, triple letters begin with AAA. There are more than 16,000 columns available in an Excel worksheet.
Cell	The intersection of a row and a column. A cell is identified by its column letter followed by its row number. For example, in Exhibit 1-1, the label "Name" is in cell A1.
Label	Text that identifies information in the spreadsheet. For example, in Exhibit 1-1, the labels in row 1 define the type of data in each column.
Value	The raw data in a spreadsheet. For example, in Exhibit 1-1, $5,767 in cell E3 is the value of third-quarter sales by Alan Monder.

Do it!

A-1: Discussing spreadsheet basics

Here's how	Here's why
1 Observe the spreadsheet shown in Exhibit 1-1	This is a list of employees and their bonus sales figures for four calendar quarters.
2 Locate the column letters	They appear across the top of the spreadsheet and identify the columns below them.
3 Locate the row numbers	They appear on the left side of the spreadsheet and identify the rows to the right of them.
4 Identify the cells	Each cell occurs at the intersection of a column and a row. Cell A1, for example, contains the text "Name."
Locate cell D4	Cell D4 is the active cell, where the insertion point is located. The column letter and row number are highlighted, and a box appears around the cell.
5 Locate the labels	Column and row labels identify information in the spreadsheet. The labels in cells A1 through G1 identify information such as name, employee number, and calendar quarter.
6 Identify the values	Values are the raw data in a spreadsheet.
7 Locate the totals	Totals are calculations based on other values in the spreadsheet. For example, cell C5 contains the total sales for the first quarter, and cell G2 contains the total sales for employee Kendra James. You use formulas to perform calculations.

Tell students that they will learn how to create formulas later.

Topic B: The Excel environment

Explanation

Excel has several interface components common to all Microsoft Office programs, as well as tools unique to Excel. The more you use these features, the more proficient you'll become at creating and modifying spreadsheets.

Starting Excel

To start Excel, click Start and choose All Programs, Microsoft Office, Microsoft Excel 2010. A new workbook called "Book1" appears in the Excel window. You can also start Excel by double-clicking an existing Excel file.

Components of the Excel window

Exhibit 1-2 shows the components of a blank workbook window, which are described in the following table.

Item	Description
Title bar	Displays the name of the workbook. "Book1" is the default name of the first workbook you start with.
Ribbon	The main location for menus and tools. Each Ribbon tab contains groups of related commands or functions.
Quick Access toolbar	Displays commands for saving the current workbook, undoing the last action, and repeating the last action. You can customize the Quick Access toolbar by adding buttons for commands that you use frequently. The Quick Access toolbar can be moved below the Ribbon.
Formula bar	Displays the contents—such as values, formulas, or labels—of the active cell. You use this bar to edit the contents of the active cell.
Worksheet	Displays rows and columns of cells. Cells can contain values, text, or formulas.
Status bar	Displays the workbook's current status. The status bar might also display information about a selected command or an operation in progress. The status bar also displays tools you can use to switch the view of the document, zoom in and out on the document, and switch to other documents.

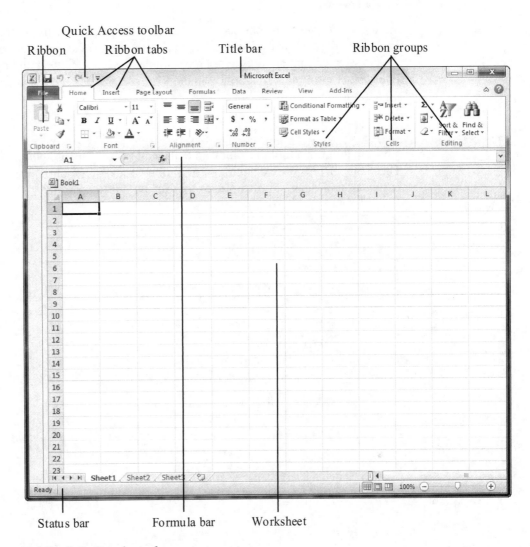

Exhibit 1-2: Excel window components

Interacting with Excel

You interact with Excel by typing and by using the mouse to choose commands, make selections, and click buttons and options.

The Ribbon interface

The *Ribbon* is the main location for menus and tools. When you click a Ribbon *tab* (such as Home, Insert, or Page Layout), the Ribbon displays separate *groups* of related tools. For example, Exhibit 1-2 points to the Styles, Cells, and Editing groups on the Home tab. Some tools are buttons you click to take an immediate action, while others expand to display menus, lists, or galleries with more options. (A *gallery* is a collection of style options that are represented graphically to provide a simple preview.)

The File tab works differently than the other tabs on the Ribbon. The File tab opens *Backstage view*, which displays a menu of commonly used file-management commands, such as Open, Save As, New, and Print.

Live Preview

With *Live Preview*, you can see the result of formatting options before you apply them. When you point to an option in a list, that option's formatting is shown on whatever data is selected in the worksheet. For example, if you select text and then display the Font list, pointing to a font option in the list makes the selected text temporarily appear in that font.

ScreenTips

You can point to a tool to display an enhanced ScreenTip, as shown in Exhibit 1-3. These ScreenTips provide quick information about each tool. If you're not sure what a particular tool does, simply point to it to see a brief description.

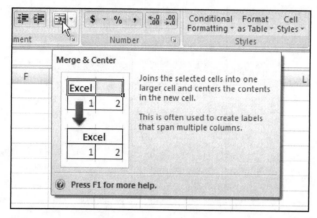

Exhibit 1-3: The Enhanced ScreenTip for the Merge & Center button

Do it!

B-1:   Examining Excel window components

If an Activation or Office Update window opens, ask students to close it.

Here's how	Here's why
1 Click **Start** and choose **All Programs**, **Microsoft Office**, **Microsoft Excel 2010**	To start Microsoft Excel.
Choose **Don't make changes** and click **OK**	(If necessary.) To close the Welcome to Microsoft Office 2010 dialog box.
2 Observe the title bar	Book1 - Microsoft Excel The title bar shows the name of the current workbook, "Book1," and the name of the program.
3 Observe the Ribbon tabs	By default, Home is active.
Observe the Home tab	The Home tab contains the Clipboard, Font, Alignment, Number, Styles, Cells, and Editing groups.
4 Click the **Insert** tab	(Next to the Home tab.) To activate it. Commands related to the Insert command are displayed here.
In the Illustrations group, click **Shapes**	To display the Shapes gallery. You can select a shape and then click a cell to place the shape there.
5 Click the **Home** tab	To display the Home tab's groups again.
6 In the Font group, point to **B**	(The Bold button.) A ScreenTip appears, showing the command name, its keyboard shortcut, and a brief description.
7 Observe the formula bar	(The formula bar is below the Ribbon.) The formula bar displays the data in the active cell. Currently, none of the cells contain data.
8 Observe the status bar	(At the bottom of the Excel window.) The status bar provides information about selected commands and the current status of the workbook. The status bar also contains tools for switching the view of the current document, zooming in and out on the current document, and switching to other documents.

Topic C: Getting help

Explanation

Excel provides a comprehensive Help system to support you as you work. You can use the Help window while offline (to open Help files located on your hard disk) or while connected to the Internet (to display Help and other resources from the Microsoft Web site).

The Excel Help window

The Help system provides assistance and information on practically all Excel-related topics. You can use it to search for specific content by using keywords or by selecting from a list of topics in the table of contents.

To open the Help window, click the question-mark icon in the upper-right corner of the Excel window, or press F1. Exhibit 1-4 shows links to various Help topics.

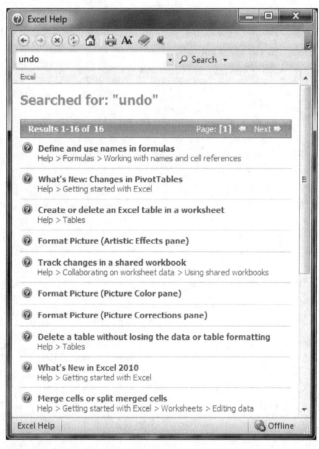

Exhibit 1-4: The Help window

When the Excel Help window opens, it connects to Office.com, by default, to display the latest information on Excel. You can browse these online Help resources, or browse the local Help files that are included when you install the program. To browse your local Help files, click the down-arrow next to Search in the Excel Help window. Under "Content from this computer," choose Excel Help. A list of broad topics is displayed. You can click a topic to drill down to more specific topics, or enter search terms in the Search box at the top of the window.

Do it!   **C-1: Getting help with using Excel**

Here's how	Here's why
1 Click [?]	(The Microsoft Excel Help button is in the top-right corner of the window.) To open the Excel Help window.
Click the arrow to the right of Search	
Under "Content from this computer," select **Excel Help**	You'll search for Help topics in the local Help system on your PC.
2 In the Search box, type **new features**	You'll search for topics about features that are new in Excel 2010.
Click **Search**	To start the search. A list of topics about new features is displayed.
3 Click the first topic in the list	A long list of topics is displayed. You can scroll down and click a topic for more information.
4 Click as shown	
	To display the Table of Contents.
5 In the Table of Contents, click **Worksheets**	The icon next to the topic changes from a closed book to an open book, and a list of subtopics is displayed.
Click **Entering data**	Another set of subtopics is displayed.
Click **Wrap text in a cell**	(Scroll down, if necessary.) Information on this topic is displayed.
6 Close the Excel Help window	Click the Close button (the X) in the upper-right corner of the window.

TIPS ✓ *Students can also press Enter after typing the search term.*

If the Table of Contents is already open, point out that the icon appears as an open book.

Topic D: Navigating a worksheet

This topic covers the following Microsoft Office Specialist objectives for exam 77-882: Excel 2010.

#	Objective
1.1	**Navigate through a worksheet**
	1.1.1 Use hot keys

Moving around in worksheets

Explanation

To begin working in an Excel file, you first need to open it. Outside Excel, you can open a file by double-clicking its icon. To open a workbook from within Excel, click the File tab. If you recently opened the file, you can click Recent and then click the file name to open the file. Otherwise, click Open on the File tab; then select the workbook you want and click Open (or double-click the workbook name).

At any given time, one cell in the worksheet is the active cell. The active cell is where the data you enter will appear. The address of the active cell appears in the Name box, to the left of the formula bar.

Objective 1.1.1

There are several ways you can move around in a worksheet. Some navigation methods make a different cell active, while others move only your view of the worksheet, without activating a different cell. The following table summarizes various worksheet navigation methods.

Action	Result
Click a cell	Selects that cell.
Press an arrow key	Selects an adjacent cell.
Press Tab	Selects the cell one column to the right.
Press Shift+Tab	Selects the cell one column to the left.
Press Ctrl+Home	Selects cell A1.
Press Ctrl+End	Selects the cell at the intersection of the last row and last column of data in a worksheet.
Click the scroll arrow	Moves the view of the worksheet one row or column. This does not change the active cell.
Click in the scrollbar	Moves the view of the worksheet one screen up, down, left, or right, depending on which side of the scroll box you click (and in which scrollbar). This does not change the active cell.
Drag the scroll box	Moves the view of the worksheet quickly without changing the active cell.
Press Ctrl+G (or choose Edit, Go To)	Opens a dialog box where you can enter the address of a cell you want to move to.
Drag the slider on the zoom bar	Zooms in or out on the current document. The zoom bar is located on the status bar, near the bottom-right corner of the window.

Do it!

D-1: Navigating a worksheet

The files for this activity are in Student Data folder **Unit 1\Topic D**.

Objective 1.1.1

TIPS *Students can also press Ctrl+O to display the Open dialog box.*

The Desktop option might not be visible until you scroll up.

Help students navigate to the current unit and topic folder, if necessary.

TIPS *Students can also double-click the file.*

Tell students that if A1 is not the active cell, they should click A1 or press Ctrl+Home.

Here's how	Here's why
1 Click the **File** tab	(The green tab on the left side of the Ribbon.) To display a menu of commonly used file-management commands, such as Open, Save As, New, and Print.
Click **Open**	To display the Open dialog box.
2 In the Navigation pane, scroll up	(If necessary.) Use the scrollbar on the left side.
Click **Desktop**	To view the folders on the desktop.
Double-click **Student Data**	Scroll down in the content pane, if necessary.
3 Navigate to the current unit and topic folder and select **Employee info**	The address bar at the top of the Open dialog box displays your current location.
Click **Open**	To open the workbook.
4 Observe the active cell	It is the cell with the outline—in this case, A1.
Observe the Name box	(The Name box is on the left side of the formula bar.) It shows the address of the active cell, A1.
5 Press [↓]	(The Down Arrow key.) To move down one row. The active cell is now A2.
Press [↑]	To move up one row. Now the active cell is A1.
6 Click the down scroll arrow, as shown	This moves your view of the window down a row, but does not change the active cell.
Drag the vertical scroll box down	(The vertical scroll box is in the right-hand scrollbar.) To quickly change your view of the worksheet without changing the active cell.
Scroll to the top of the worksheet	

TIPS *Tell students they can also press Ctrl+G.*

7	On the Home tab, in the Editing group, click **Find & Select**	The Editing group is on the far right side of the Ribbon.
	Choose **Go To...**	To open the Go To dialog box. You'll use it to move to a specific cell in the worksheet.
	Type **A43** and click **OK**	(In the Reference box.) To move to cell A43, the last data row in the worksheet.
8	Press (CTRL) + (HOME)	To return to cell A1.
9	Press (CTRL) + (END)	To move to the intersection of the last row and last column of data in the worksheet. This is useful for moving to the end of a list of data so that you can enter more data.
	Return to cell A1	Press Ctrl+Home.
10	Drag the zoom slider to the left	(The zoom slider is in the status bar, in the lower-right corner of the window.) To see all of the data in this worksheet without scrolling.

For 1024×768 resolution, this will be approximately 60%. For 800×600 resolution, this will be about 45%.

Students' zoom percentages might differ from what is shown here.

	Continue dragging until rows 1–43 in the worksheet are visible	
	Click the percentage number on the zoom bar	To open the Zoom dialog box.
	Select **100%** and click **OK**	To return to 100% magnification.
11	Experiment with various navigation techniques	You can use the table preceding this activity as a guide.
12	Press (CTRL) + (HOME)	To make A1 the active cell again.

If a message box appears, asking if students want to save the workbook, tell them to click Don't Save.

13	Click the **File** tab and then click **Close**	To close the workbook. (If prompted, don't save your changes.)

Unit summary: Getting started

Topic A   In this topic, you learned that **spreadsheets** can help you organize, calculate, and analyze data. You also learned about the common features of all spreadsheets, which include rows, columns, cells, values, labels, and formulas.

Topic B   In this topic, you identified components of the Excel interface, and you learned how to work with tools on the **Ribbon**, which is divided into tabs and groups. You learned that you can get information about a command by pointing to it.

Topic C   In this topic, you learned how to use the **Help** system to get information about Excel tools and techniques.

Topic D   In this topic, you learned how to open an Excel file, identify the **active cell**, and navigate through a worksheet by using the keyboard and the mouse.

Independent practice activity

In this activity, you'll open an Excel file, navigate in that file, use Help, and close the file.

The files for this activity are in Student Data folder **Unit 1\Unit summary**.

1 Open the file Employee details.

2 Activate cell B30.

3 Use Help to get information on saving a file.

4 Use the Find & Select group to navigate to F23. Return to A1.

5 Close Employee details. If prompted to save changes, click No.

6 Close Excel.

Review questions

1 What is the difference between a worksheet and a workbook?

   A worksheet consists of rows and columns that intersect to form cells that contain various kinds of data. A workbook consists of multiple worksheets. By default, each workbook contains three worksheets.

2 What is a Ribbon group?

   A Ribbon group is a collection of related tools on a Ribbon tab.

3 What is an active cell?

   The active cell is where the data you enter will appear.

4 What key combination would you use to return to cell A1?

   Ctrl+Home.

5 What key combination would you use to go directly to the last row of data in a worksheet?

   Ctrl+End.

6 What menu command or key combination would you use to move to a specific cell that is at the far end of the current worksheet?

   Click Find & Select and Go To, or press Ctrl+G, to open a dialog box where you can enter the address of the cell you want to move to.

Unit 2

Entering and editing data

Unit time: 45 minutes

Complete this unit, and you'll know how to:

A Create an Excel workbook, and enter and edit text and values in a worksheet.

B Enter and edit formulas in a worksheet.

C Insert, move, and resize pictures in a worksheet.

D Save and update a workbook, and save a workbook as a PDF.

Topic A: Entering and editing text and values

This topic covers the following Microsoft Office Specialist objectives for exam 77-882: Excel 2010.

#	Objective
2.2	**Apply AutoFill**
	2.2.2 Fill a series
2.1	**Construct cell data**
	2.1.4 Select cell data

Text and values

Explanation

As soon as you create a workbook, you can begin entering data in cells. Cell entries can include many types of data, including text and values. When you type, data is entered in the active cell.

Text in cells can be any length, and you can change the text's formatting, such as its font and size. By default, text in a cell is left-aligned, as shown in Exhibit 2-1.

Values can include numbers, formulas, and functions. (Formulas and functions are explained in detail later.) Excel recognizes cell data as a value when it's a number or when it begins with +, -, =, @, #, or $. By default, a value in a cell is right-aligned.

	A	B	C	D	E	F
1	**Outlander Spices**					
2	**Bonus sales for the northern region**					
3						
4						
5						
6	Name	Emp #	Qtr1	Qtr2	Qtr3	Qtr4
7	Kendra James	16	$6,354	$4,846	$3,958	$8,284
8	Alan Monder	22	$7,546	$6,574	$5,767	$6,234
9	Audrey Kress	27	$7,635	$4,765	$5,256	$7,865
10	Julie George	29	$9,595	$5,859	$4,879	$3,432

Exhibit 2-1: A sample worksheet with text and values

Overflowing text and values

If your text doesn't fit in a cell, it will appear to go into the next cell if that adjacent cell is empty. The text isn't actually in that adjacent cell, however—if there is data in the adjacent cell, the overflowing text is truncated to fit the width of its cell.

If a long value doesn't fit in a cell, Excel displays a row of # characters. This indicates that the cell is too narrow to display the value in full, as shown in Exhibit 2-2.

The text in A1 appears to spill over into adjacent cells

The formula bar shows that D1, the active cell, is actually empty

That same text in A4 is truncated by the presence of text in B4

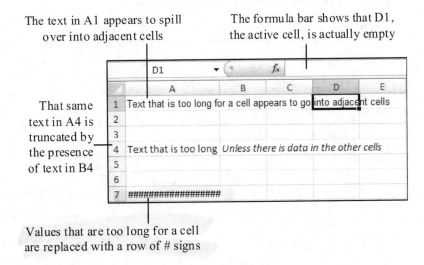

Values that are too long for a cell are replaced with a row of # signs

Exhibit 2-2: Text and values that overflow their cells

The Num Lock key (for desktop computers)

Many desktop keyboards have a numeric keypad, which is enabled and disabled by a Num Lock key in the upper-left corner of the keypad. Press Num Lock once to switch the keypad from functioning as numeric keys to functioning as navigation keys. Press Num Lock again to return to number entry. When number entry is active, a Num Lock light typically lights on the keyboard.

If you have a numeric keypad, you might find it easier to use than the standard numeric keys when entering values in Excel.

LED lit to indicate that Num Lock is active

Num Lock key

Keyboard's numeric keypad

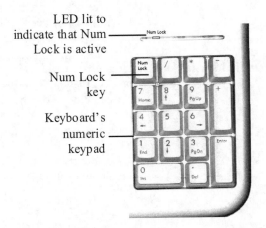

Exhibit 2-3: The Num Lock key on a desktop keyboard's numeric keypad

A-1: Entering text and values

If the Excel program shortcut is not on the Start menu, have students click Start and choose All Programs, Microsoft Office, Microsoft Excel 2010.

Tell students to keep the program window maximized for this course.

Here's how	Here's why
1 Start Excel	(Click Start and choose Microsoft Excel 2010.) The title bar displays "Book1," which is the name of the default workbook.
Maximize the Excel window	If necessary.
2 Click the **File** tab	You'll close this default workbook and then start a new one.
Choose **Close**	To close the workbook. The tools and commands are dimmed because no file is open.
3 Click the **File** tab	
Click **New**	To display the list of templates.
4 Verify that **Blank Workbook** is selected	
On the right side of the window, click **Create**	To create a new workbook. The name of the workbook, "Book2," appears in the title bar.
5 Select B1	(Click it.) To make B1 the active cell. The cell address B1 appears in the Name box.
6 Type **Outlander Spices**	To specify a heading for the worksheet. The text (or any other data) overlaps other blank cells if it takes up more room than the current cell size. However, the data is the content of only the cell where you entered it—in this case, B1.
Press ⏎ ENTER	To complete the entry and move to B2. By default, text entries are aligned to the left in their cells.
7 Select A4	
Type **Month** and press ⏎ ENTER	To create a text label and move to A5.
8 In A5, enter **January**	
9 In B4, enter **Region1**	

10 In B5, enter **21000**

	A	B	C
1		Outlander Spices	
2			
3			
4	Month	Region1	
5	January	21000	
6			

To enter the Region 1 sales figure for January.
The workbook should now look as shown here.

Editing text and values

Explanation

If you make an error while entering data in a cell, you can correct it at any time. To make edits, do any of the following:

- Select the cell and type the new data.
- Click the formula bar, make the edits, and press Enter.
- Double-click the cell to place the insertion point in it, make the desired edits, and press Enter.

Selecting multiple cells

Objective 2.1.4

If you need to select more than one cell at a time, you can hold down the Ctrl key and then click each cell to select the ones you want. If you want to select a contiguous range of cells (in a row or column), click the first cell in the range, hold down the Shift key, and then click the last cell in the range. All cells in between are selected. Or you can simply drag across cells to select them.

Do it!

A-2: Editing cell contents

Here's how	Here's why
1 In A2, enter **Extra sales projections**	
2 Select A2	You'll modify the contents of this cell.
In the formula bar, double-click **Extra**	To select it so you can edit it.
Type **Bonus**	To change the text to "Bonus sales projections."
3 Press (END)	To move the insertion point to the end of the text, where you'll add a few more words.
Press (SPACEBAR)	To add a space.
Type **for the northern region** and press (← ENTER)	The text now reads "Bonus sales projections for the northern region."
4 In A3, enter **Final Version**	
5 In C3, enter **Confidential**	
6 Select A3	You'll remove the text from A3 and C3.
Press (CTRL) and select C3	By holding down the Ctrl key, you can select multiple cells simultaneously. The outline box surrounds the current cell, while other selected cells are highlighted.

Objective 2.1.4

7 Press (← BACKSPACE)

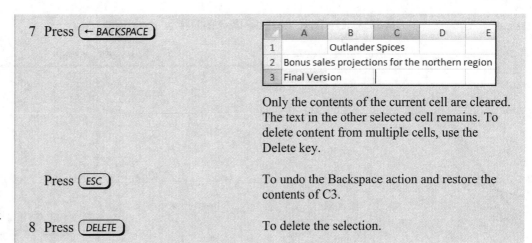

Only the contents of the current cell are cleared. The text in the other selected cell remains. To delete content from multiple cells, use the Delete key.

Press (ESC)

To undo the Backspace action and restore the contents of C3.

8 Press (DELETE)

To delete the selection.

AutoFill

Explanation

Objective 2.2.2

When you want to enter a series of numbers, days of the week, or other sequential data, you can use the AutoFill feature to complete the list. The *fill handle* is a small square in the lower-right corner of a selected cell or range of cells. When you point to the fill handle, the pointer changes to a plus sign (+). You can then drag the pointer downward to fill a range with data, as shown in Exhibit 2-4.

To use AutoFill:

1 Select the cell containing the value that will start the list or series.

2 Point to the fill handle until the pointer changes to a + symbol.

3 Drag the fill handle over the adjacent cells that you want to fill.

For numbers or dates, you can select two cells with a desired range, and AutoFill will continue with the same increments. For example, you could use this technique to fill a range by 10s or to fill a range with dates a week apart.

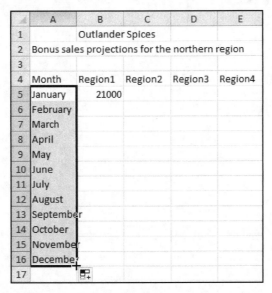

Exhibit 2-4: Using AutoFill to create a column of month labels

A-3: Using AutoFill to fill a series

Here's how	Here's why
1 Select B4	It contains the text "Region1." You'll use AutoFill to add more headings.
2 Point to the fill handle, as shown	Region1 21000 The pointer changes to a plus sign.
3 Press and hold the mouse button	
Drag the fill handle to the right, to E4, as shown	Region1 21000 Region4 As you drag, a shaded outline appears around the range you're filling. As you drag past a cell, a ScreenTip displays the text that will be entered in that cell.
Release the mouse button	To automatically fill the cells in the range.
4 Select A5	You'll AutoFill the remaining months in the year.
AutoFill to cell A16	(Drag the fill handle to A16.) The cells are populated with the months of the year.
5 Click the **File** tab and then click **Close**	To close the workbook. A message appears, prompting you to save the workbook.
Click **Don't Save**	To close the workbook without saving it.

Point out that students should AutoFill until they see December in the ScreenTip.

Topic B: Entering and editing formulas

This topic covers the following Microsoft Office Specialist objectives for exam 77-882: Excel 2010.

#	Objective
5.1	**Create formulas**
	5.1.1 Use basic operators
	5.1.2 Revise formulas
5.2	**Enforce precedence**
	5.2.1 Order of evaluation
	5.2.2 Precedence using parentheses
	5.2.3 Precedence of operators for percent vs. exponentiation
5.3	**Apply cell references in formulas**
	5.3.1 Relative and absolute references

Formulas

Explanation

Objective 5.1.1

Formulas perform numeric calculations, such as adding, multiplying, and averaging. All formulas in Excel start with the equal sign (=). A formula can refer to a value, a cell address, or another formula. *Functions* are predefined formulas that perform operations or calculations, from simple to complex. Many formulas contain *operators*—characters that indicate the type of arithmetic operation the formula will perform.

The following table shows some common arithmetic operators you can use.

Operator	Used for...	Example
+	Addition	=A7+A9
-	Subtraction	=A7-A9
*	Multiplication	=A7*A9
/	Division	=A7/A9
%	Percentages	=50%
^	Exponents	=5^3 means 5 raised to the third power (5^3), or 5*5*5

Entering formulas

Objective 5.3.1

To enter a formula, select the cell where you want the result to appear, type the formula, and press Enter. For example, if there are number values in A2 and A3, and you want to add them and show the result in A4, you select A4, type =A2+A3, and press Enter. The sum will appear in A4. If A4 is the active cell, the formula appears in the formula bar, as shown in Exhibit 2-5.

Formulas are based on the values contained in the cells in your worksheet. If you change the value in a cell that a formula refers to, the result of the formula will change to reflect the new value.

A4	▼	f_x	=A2+A3
	A	B	C	D
1				
2	44			
3	66			
4	110			
5				

Exhibit 2-5: A sum shown in the cell while the formula is shown in the formula bar

Do it!

B-1:   Creating a basic formula

The files for this activity are in Student Data folder **Unit 2\Topic B**.

Objectives 5.1.1, 5.3.1

Here's how	Here's why
1 On the File tab, click **Open**	The Open dialog box appears.
Open **Sales**	Navigate to Student Data folder Unit 2\Topic B, if necessary, and double-click Sales.
2 Select G5	You'll enter a formula in this cell.
Type **=**	All formulas begin with an equal sign.
3 Type **C5+D5+E5+F5**	This formula adds the values of the quarterly bonus sales for Kendra James; these values are in cells C5 through F5.
Press (← ENTER)	The result of the formula is $23,442.00.
4 Select G5	f_x | =C5+D5+E5+F5
	The formula bar shows the formula, not the result.
5 Select F5	You'll change the value in this cell.
Type **1000**	
Press (← ENTER)	The result of the formula in G5 automatically changes to $16,158.00.

Help students open the file if necessary.

⚠ *Tell students not to press Enter after typing the equal sign.*

Point out that it's not necessary for students to capitalize the column letters as they type. Excel will do that automatically when they press Enter.

Tell students that the decimal will automatically be placed correctly.

Using the mouse to enter cell references in formulas

Explanation

You can use the mouse to enter cell references for a formula. To do so:

1 Select the cell where you want to enter the formula.
2 Type = (to begin a formula).
3 Click the cell for which you want to enter a reference.
4 Type the operator you want.
5 Repeat Steps 3 and 4 until your formula is complete.
6 Press Enter.

Do it!

B-2: Entering cell references with the mouse

Here's how	Here's why
1 Select G6	You'll enter a formula to calculate the total quarterly bonus sales for Pamela Carter.
Type =	To begin the formula.
2 Select C6	To enter this cell's address in the formula you're creating.
Type +	To continue to build the formula.
3 Select D6	
4 Complete the formula as shown, using the mouse to enter the cell addresses	f_x =C6+D6+E6+F6
Press (↵ ENTER)	To enter the formula. G6 now contains the total quarterly bonus sales figure for Pamela Carter. G9 contains $40,913.00, which is the total of the values in G5 and G6.
5 In G7, enter a formula to calculate the total bonus sales for Julie George	Use whichever method you prefer. When you are finished, G7 should contain $23,765.

Editing formulas

Explanation

Objective 5.1.2

You can edit formulas to adapt to changes in the worksheet or to correct mistakes. You edit a formula just as you would edit any other cell. Simply double-click the cell and enter the correct formula. You can also click a cell to select it, edit the formula in the formula bar, and press Enter.

Do it!

Objective 5.1.2

B-3: Editing a formula

Here's how	Here's why
1 Observe G9	The total in this cell is incorrect.
2 Select G9	You'll edit the formula in this cell.
Observe the formula bar	The formula bar shows =G5+G6, which doesn't include the total for Julie George.
3 Place the insertion point at the end of the formula	⊗ ✕ ✓ *fx* =G5+G6
4 Type **+G7**	To add the value in G7 to the formula.
Press ⏎ ENTER	
5 Observe G9	G9 now shows the correct value, $64,678.00.
6 Click the **File** tab and then click **Close**	To close the workbook. A message appears, prompting you to save the workbook.
Click **Don't Save**	To close the workbook without saving it.

The order of evaluation

Explanation

Objectives 5.2.1–5.2.3

When a formula contains more than one arithmetic operator, Excel performs the calculations in the following order:

1 Percentages

2 Exponents

3 Multiplication and division

4 Addition and subtraction

When operators with the same precedence, such as multiplication and division, appear in the same formula, Excel performs those calculations from left to right.

Using parentheses to change the order

You can change the order in which the operations are calculated by placing parentheses around the part of the formula you want to be calculated first.

Do it!

B-4:   Working with the order of operations

The files for this activity are in Student Data folder **Unit 2\Topic B**.

Objectives 5.2.1, 5.2.2

Here's how	Here's why
1 Click the **File** tab	
Open Profit	Navigate to the current topic folder, select Profit, and click Open.
2 In F5, type **=B5−C5*D5−E5**	To calculate the profit for chive sales, you'll subtract the quantity on hand from the starting quantity, then multiply by the sales price and subtract the cost.

Explain how the order of operations affected the profit number.

Press (⏎ ENTER)	f_x =B5-C5*D5-E5
	The result is 6.20 because of the order in which the operators are handled. The multiplication operator is calculated first, so C5*D5 is 195. This result subtracted from B5 is 7. And finally, E5 is subtracted, and the result is 6.20.
3 Click in the formula bar	To edit the formula.
4 Place the insertion point at the beginning of the formula	✗ ✔ f_x =B5-C5*D5-E5
5 Type **(**	
Place insertion point after C5, and type **)**	✗ ✔ f_x =(B5-C5)*D5-E5
	To enclose the first subtraction operator in parentheses.
6 Enclose the second subtraction operator in parentheses	✗ ✔ f_x =(B5-C5)*(D5-E5)
Press (⏎ ENTER)	Profit 50.40
	The profit has been calculated correctly and 50.40 is displayed in F5.

Objective 5.2.3

7 In any empty cell below row 9, enter **=6*50%^2**	

Point out that this simple example is used to demonstrate how Excel calculates percentages before exponents.

Why is the result 1.5 and not 9?	Excel calculates the formula in the following order: 50% is converted to .5; then .5 raised to the power of 2 is .25; and finally, .25 multiplied by 6 is 1.5.
8 Close the workbook without saving it	Click the File tab and click Close. When prompted to save your changes, click Don't Save.

Topic C: Working with pictures

This topic covers the following Microsoft Office Specialist objectives for exam 77-882: Excel 2010.

#	Objective
6.2	**Apply and manipulate illustrations**
	6.2.1 Insert
	6.2.2 Position
	6.2.3 Size
	6.2.4 Rotate

Adding images to a worksheet

Explanation

You can insert images in your Excel files to illustrate and enhance worksheets and printed reports. Excel supports dozens of industry-standard image file formats, including .bmp, .jpg, .eps, and .tif.

To add an image to a worksheet:

Objective 6.2.1

1 Click the Insert tab.
2 In the Illustrations group, click Picture to open the Insert Picture dialog box.
3 Navigate to the picture's location, select the file, and click Insert. The picture appears in the worksheet, and the Picture Tools | Format tab is activated.
4 Use the tools on the Format tab to modify the picture as necessary.

	A	B	C	D	E	F	G
1			Outlander Spices				
2			**Bonus sales in the northern region**				
3							
4	Name	Emp #	Qtr1	Qtr2	Qtr3	Qtr4	Total
5	Kendra James	16	$6,354.00	$4,846.00	$3,958.00	$8,284.00	$23,442.00
6	Pamela Carter	25	$8,484.00	$5,858.00	$5,858.00	$4,555.00	$24,755.00
7	Julie George	29	$9,595.00	$5,859.00	$4,879.00	$3,432.00	$23,765.00

Exhibit 2-6: A worksheet with a picture

Moving images on a worksheet

Objective 6.2.2

When you insert an image in a worksheet, Excel places it in the approximate middle of your screen. You can then move the image so that it appears and prints where you want it. To move an image:

1   Point anywhere within the picture. The pointer changes to a four-headed arrow.

2   Drag the picture. As you drag, the picture remains stationary, but a transparent copy of it moves with the pointer, as shown in Exhibit 2-7.

3   Place the transparent copy where you want the picture to be.

4   Release the mouse button. The picture moves to that location on the worksheet.

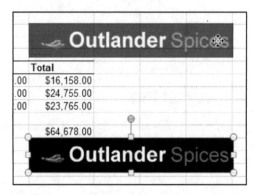

Exhibit 2-7: Moving an image

Resizing images

There are several ways to resize a picture:

Objective 6.2.3

- Select the picture to activate the Picture Tools | Format tab. In the Size group, enter new values in the Height and Width boxes.

- In the Size group, click the Dialog Box Launcher button (in the lower-right corner of the group). The Format Picture dialog box opens, showing size-related options. Under Size and Rotate (or under Scale), change the values as needed.

- Point to one of the sizing handles at the corners of the picture frame. The pointer changes to a double-headed arrow. Drag a sizing handle to resize the picture.

To resize a picture proportionally, hold down the Shift key before dragging the sizing handles. This forces the picture's height and width to retain their relative proportions.

Rotating images

Objective 6.2.4

There are several ways to rotate a picture:

- Select the picture to activate the Picture Tools | Format tab. In the Arrange group, click Rotate. You can rotate the picture 90 degrees to the left or to the right. You can also flip the picture horizontally or vertically.

- From the Rotate gallery, choose More Rotation Options. Use the Rotation box to specify an exact angle in degrees, and then click Close.

- Point to the green rotation handle above the picture. The pointer changes to a circular arrow. Drag to rotate the picture.

Undo

If you make a mistake in Excel, it is easy to reverse. Simply click the Undo button on the Quick Access toolbar, or press Ctrl+Z.

Do it!

C-1:   Inserting and modifying a picture

The files for this activity are in Student Data folder **Unit 2\Topic C**.

Here's how	Here's why
1 Open Sales 2	From the current topic folder.
2 Click the **Insert** tab	You'll insert a logo image in this worksheet.
3 Click ![Picture icon]	(The Insert Picture From File button is in the Illustrations group.) The Insert Picture dialog box opens.
Navigate to the current unit and topic folder	
Select **logo** and click **Insert**	To insert the picture. The logo appears in the middle of the worksheet, and the Picture Tools | Format tab is activated.
4 In the Size group, observe the picture dimensions	![Size group showing 0.49" height and 3.02" width] The picture is 0.49 inches tall and 3.02 inches wide.
5 Point to the handle in the lower-right corner of the picture, as shown	![Spices logo with resize handle] The pointer changes to a double-headed arrow.
Press and hold (SHIFT)	
Drag up and to the left slightly	To proportionally resize the picture.
6 Observe the picture dimensions	In the Size group.
Resize the picture proportionally to fill the height of three rows	Press Shift and drag the picture handle in or out to get the desired size.

Objective 6.2.1

TIPS *Students can also double-click the logo to insert it.*

Objective 6.2.3

The picture size does not need to be exact.

Objective 6.2.4

7 Point to the rotation handle above the picture, as shown

The pointer changes to a circular arrow.

Drag to rotate the picture

As you drag the green rotation handle, the picture rotates on an axis.

Click [⤺]

To undo your last action and return the picture to its original angle.

Objective 6.2.2

8 Point anywhere inside the picture

The pointer changes to a four-headed arrow.

Drag up and to the left

A transparent copy of the picture moves with the pointer.

Place the upper-left corner of the picture in B1

Where the text "Outlander Spices" is displayed.

9 Click anywhere in the worksheet

To deselect the picture.

⚠ *Tell students to close the file but not Excel.*

10 Close the file without saving your changes

Click the File tab, click Close, and then click Don't Save.

Topic D: Saving and updating workbooks

This topic covers the following Microsoft Office Specialist objectives for exam 77-882: Excel 2010.

#	Objective
7.1	**Share spreadsheets by using Backstage**
	7.1.2 Change the file type to a different version of Excel
	7.1.3 Save as PDF or XPS

The Save As dialog box

Explanation

Saving a workbook stores your data for future use. Every time you change anything in a worksheet, you'll need to save it (update it) if you want to keep your changes.

The first time you save a workbook, you use the Save As dialog box to assign a file name and location to the file. You can also use the Save As dialog box to create a new file based on your current file.

When you save a file, it's an Excel workbook by default. However, you can also save it in a variety of formats, including those in the following table.

Format	Extension	Description
Excel Workbook	.xlsx	This is the default workbook format for Excel 2010.
Excel 97-2003 Workbook	.xls	This workbook format can be opened by earlier versions of Excel.
XML Data	.xml	The XML format is useful for data that must be transferred between applications.
Text (Tab delimited)	.txt	Files saved in plain text format can be opened by any word processor or text editor. Values are delimited (separated) by tabs.
CSV (Comma delimited)	.csv	Data fields in a CSV file are delimited by commas.
PDF	.pdf	This option saves the file in the popular Adobe PDF format so that anyone with the free Adobe Reader program can open the file.
Web Page	.html	This format enables the workbook to be published as a Web page.

To save a workbook for the first time, or to save an existing file with a new name:

1   Click the File tab and then choose Save As to open the Save As dialog box.
2   In the File name box, enter a name for the workbook.
3   Select the location where you want to save the workbook.
4   If you want to save the file in a format other than an Excel workbook, select a file format from the "Save as type" list.
5   Click Save.

Do it!

D-1: Saving a new workbook

Here's how	Here's why
1 Press CTRL + N	To create a new workbook.
2 Click 🖫	(The Save button is on the Quick Access toolbar, in the top-left corner of the application window.) To save the workbook. The Save As dialog box opens because this file is new and does not yet have a name.
In the File name box, enter **My new file**	File name: My new file Save as type: Excel Workbook
Navigate to the current topic folder	In the address bar, at the top of the Save As dialog box, you can click the arrow next to the current unit and select the current topic.
Click **Save**	
3 Observe the title bar	The new file name is displayed.
4 Click the **File** tab	
Click **Close**	To close the new file.

TIPS ✔ *Students can also click the File tab and then click New.*

Help students navigate to the current topic folder, if necessary.

TIPS ✔ *Students can also press Enter after typing the file name.*

Saving files for a previous version of Excel

Explanation

Objective 7.1.2

Workbooks created in Excel 2010 are compatible with Excel 2007 files but not with Excel 97-2003 workbook files. You can, however, save a workbook created in Excel 2010 as an Excel 97-2003 workbook to enable people with earlier versions to open and use it.

To save a workbook in the Excel 97-2003 Workbook format, click the File tab and click Save As. In the Save As dialog box, select Excel 97-2003 Workbook from the "Save as type" list. Enter a name for the workbook, if necessary, and click Save.

Note: Not all features present in Excel 2010 workbooks can be saved in the 97-2003 workbook format. You can check which features are compatible with earlier versions of Excel by running the Compatibility Checker. On the File tab, click Info. Click the Check for Issues button and choose Check Compatibility.

Do it!

D-2: Saving a file as an Excel 97-2003 workbook

The files for this activity are in Student Data folder **Unit 2\Topic D**.

Objective 7.1.2

Here's how	Here's why
1 Open 2003 Sales	From the current topic folder.
2 Click the **File** tab	
3 Click **Save As**	You'll save this worksheet as an Excel 97-2003 Workbook file.
4 In the File name box, enter **My 2003 Sales**	File name: My 2003 Sales
5 From the "Save as type" list, select **Excel 97-2003 Workbook**	Save as type: Excel Workbook Authors: Excel Workbook / Excel Macro-Enabled Workbook / Excel Binary Workbook / Excel 97-2003 Workbook / XML Data
Verify that the current unit and topic folders are selected	
6 Click **Save**	To save the file as a 97-2003 workbook with a new name.
Close the workbook	

TIPS *Students can also press F12 to open the Save As dialog box.*

Saving a worksheet as a PDF file

Explanation

Objective 7.1.3

PDF (Portable Document Format) is a popular format for sharing documents of all kinds. Using PDF for document sharing means that people you share the file with don't need to have a copy of the authoring application to open and read the file. So, for example, you can save a spreadsheet as a PDF document and share it with someone who does not have Microsoft Excel.

To save a worksheet as a PDF file:

1 With the worksheet open, click the File tab and then click Save As.

2 In the File name box, enter a name for the file (or use the current file name).

3 From the "Save as type" list, select PDF.

4 Click Save. Excel converts the active worksheet to PDF and saves it, and the worksheet remains open in Excel.

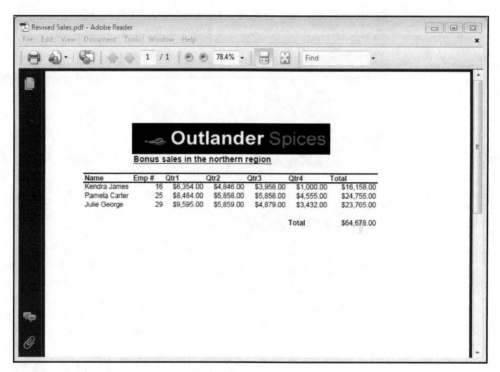

Exhibit 2-8: The Excel worksheet as a PDF file

Do it!

D-3: Saving a worksheet as a PDF file

The files for this activity are in Student Data folder **Unit 2\Topic D**.

Objective 7.1.3

Here's how	Here's why
1 Open Revised Sales	From the current topic folder.
2 Open the Save As dialog box	(Click the File tab and click Save As.) You'll save this worksheet as a PDF file.
Verify that the address bar displays the current topic folder	Navigate to the current topic folder if necessary.
3 From the "Save as type" list, select **PDF**	You'll keep the current file name.
Verify that **Open file after publishing** is checked	☑ Open file after publishing
Click **Save**	Excel converts the active worksheet to PDF and opens it in Adobe Reader, as shown in Exhibit 2-8. The worksheet (in Excel format) remains open.
4 Observe the PDF	(If a License Agreement dialog box appears, click Accept.) Adobe Reader is available as a free download from the Adobe Web site. You could share this file with people who need the worksheet but don't have Excel.
5 Close Adobe Reader	
6 Save the workbook as **My Revised Sales**	Save the file as an Excel workbook in the current topic folder.

Help students with this step, if necessary.

Have students check it if it's not already checked.

If the PDF does not open, have students minimize Excel and open the PDF from the desktop.

Updating a workbook

Explanation

Each time you save a workbook, Excel updates the workbook file with the latest changes. You should update your workbooks frequently so that your changes aren't lost. To save changes in a workbook, click the Save button on the Quick Access toolbar or press Ctrl+S.

Do it!

D-4: Editing and updating a workbook

Excel is active and Revised Sales is open.

Here's how	Here's why
1 In A10, enter **Annual target**	To edit the worksheet.
2 Click 🖫	(The Save button.) To update the workbook with the new text.
3 Change the value in C5 to **8000**	
4 Press CTRL + S	To update the workbook.
5 Close the workbook	Click the File tab and click Close.

Unit summary: Entering and editing data

Topic A   In this topic, you created a **workbook**, and you entered and edited **text** and **values** in a worksheet. You learned how to edit a cell by using the formula bar and by double-clicking a cell. You also learned how to select multiple cells and **AutoFill** a series.

Topic B   In this topic, you learned how to use **formulas** to perform calculations on values in a worksheet. You learned how to enter formulas and how to use an **operator** to combine values. You also learned how to use the mouse to enter **cell references** and how to edit formulas. You also examined the **order of operations** and how it affects calculation results.

Topic C   In this topic, you learned how to insert a **picture** into a worksheet. You also learned how to resize a picture proportionally and move a picture in the worksheet.

Topic D   In this topic, you learned how to **save** and update a workbook, and you learned how to save a file with a new name and in a different location. You also learned how to save a worksheet as a **PDF** file.

Independent practice activity

In this activity, you'll create a workbook, enter data, create formulas, save the workbook, and save it as a PDF.

The files for this activity are in Student Data folder **Unit 2\Unit summary**.

1 Create a new workbook.

2 Enter data beginning in row 4, as shown in Exhibit 2-9.

3 In column E, enter formulas to calculate the total costs for each item. (*Hint:* The multiplication operator is *.) Compare your results to Exhibit 2-10.

4 Insert the picture file **Outlander** into the worksheet.

5 Resize the picture and position it as shown in Exhibit 2-10. (*Hint:* Resize the picture proportionally until it's approximately 1.65 inches wide.)

6 Save the workbook as **My costs** in Student Data folder Unit 2\Unit summary.

7 Save the workbook as a PDF file.

8 Close Adobe Reader and close the workbook.

	A	B	C	D	E
1					
2					
3					
4	Code	Desc	Quantity	Cost/Item	Total cost
5					
6	10001	Garlic	16	2.5	
7	12001	Cayenne	7	4	
8	13003	Dill	5	6	
9					

Exhibit 2-9: The data to be entered in Step 2

	A	B	C	D	E
1					
2	**Outlander**				
3					
4	Code	Desc	Quantity	Cost/Item	Total cost
5					
6	10001	Garlic	16	2.5	40
7	12001	Cayenne	7	4	28
8	13003	Dill	5	6	30

Exhibit 2-10: The formula results after Step 4

Review questions

1 Name two basic types of data that can be entered in a worksheet.

You can enter text or values. Values can be numbers, formulas, or functions.

2 If the text you enter into a cell is longer than the width of the cell, what happens?

It will appear to go into the next cell if that adjacent cell is empty.

3 If the text you enter into a cell is longer than the width of the cell, and the adjacent cell is not empty, what happens?

The overflowing text is truncated to fit the width of its cell.

4 If you enter a value into a cell that is longer than the width of the cell, what happens?

A row of # characters is displayed in the cell.

5 All formulas must begin with what symbol?

All formulas begin with the equal sign (=).

6 How do you resize a picture so that its dimensions remain proportional?

Press Shift and drag one of the resizing handles on the picture.

7 Why might you want to save a workbook as a PDF?

So that people can view the workbook even if they don't have Excel. Adobe Reader is a free download from the Adobe Web site.

Unit 3

Modifying a worksheet

Unit time: 50 minutes

Complete this unit, and you'll know how to:

A Move and copy data in a worksheet.

B Move and copy formulas in a worksheet.

C Use absolute references in formulas.

D Insert and delete ranges, rows, and columns in a worksheet.

Topic A: Moving and copying data

This topic covers the following Microsoft Office Specialist objectives for exam 77-882: Excel 2010.

#	Objective
2.1	**Construct cell data**
	2.1.1 Use Paste Special
	2.1.1.1 Formats
	2.1.1.3 Values
	2.1.1.4 Preview icons
	2.1.2 Cut
	2.1.3 Move

Moving data

Explanation

You can move and copy data between cells, ranges, and worksheets, and even from one workbook to another. When you cut or copy data, Excel places it on the Clipboard, an area of memory that stores data temporarily. You can then "paste" the data from the Clipboard into a new location.

You can move data by clicking the Home tab and using the Cut and Paste buttons in the Clipboard group. Here's how:

Objectives 2.1.2, 2.1.3

1   Select the cell containing the data you want to move.
2   Click the Home tab, if necessary.
3   In the Clipboard group, click Cut (or press Crtl+X).
4   Select the cell that you want to move the data to.
5   In the Clipboard group, click Paste (or press Ctrl+V).

You use Cut (or Ctrl+X) only to move a cell's data, not to delete the data. Data that has been cut is not removed from the original cell until it's pasted into another cell.

Do it!

A-1: Moving data in a worksheet

The files for this activity are in Student Data folder **Unit 3\Topic A**.

Objectives 2.1.2, 2.1.3

Here's how	Here's why
1 Open Data	
Save the workbook as **My Data**	You'll modify the data in this workbook.
2 Select F12	You'll move the contents of this cell.
On the Home tab, click ✂	(The Cut button is in the Clipboard group.) To cut the contents of F12.
Observe the marquee around F12	‚National Sales‚
	The moving, dashed boundary indicates that you have cut the cell data, and it's now on the Clipboard.
3 Select F4	To select the new location for the data.
Click 📋	(The Paste button is in the Clipboard group.) To paste the contents of F12 into F4. F12 is now empty.
4 Select D7	You'll move only part of the text in this cell.
5 In the formula bar, select **and Marketing**, as shown	
	You also need to select the space before "and."
Press CTRL + X	To cut the selected text from D7.
Observe the formula bar	*fx* Sales
	The selected text has been removed from D7.
6 Select D12	You'll paste the text at the end of the text in this cell.
Place the insertion point as shown	X ✓ *fx* Sales
Press CTRL + V	To paste the text into D12.
7 Click 💾	To save the workbook.

TIPS *Students can also press Ctrl+X.*

TIPS *Students can also press Ctrl+V.*

Tell students to select backwards, starting with the end of Marketing, to more easily select the space before the "and."

Copying data

Explanation

Objective 2.2.1

When you need to use the same data in several places, it's best to copy it (for accuracy), rather than type it repeatedly at each location. You can copy data within a worksheet, between worksheets, between workbooks, and among other applications. You can copy all or part of a cell's contents, or the content in a range of cells.

To copy data:

1   Select the data you want to copy.

2   In the Clipboard group on the Home tab, click Copy (or press Ctrl+C).

Pasting data

To paste data:

1   Select the destination cell.

2   In the Clipboard group, click Paste (or press Ctrl+V).

Using Paste Special

*Objectives 2.1.1.1,
2.1.1.4*

To control what is being pasted, click the arrow on the Paste button to display the Paste Options menu. For example, you can paste only the text, the text and its formatting, or only the formatting of the copied cell. You can point to the Paste Special icons to see a preview of the pasted result in the destination cell.

In addition, when you paste the copied data, the Paste Options button appears next to the destination cell. You can click this button or press the Ctrl key to display the Paste Options shortcut menu.

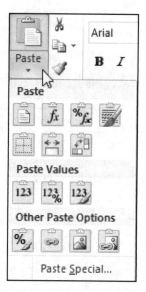

Exhibit 3-1: The paste options

Do it!

A-2:   Copying data in a worksheet

Here's how	Here's why
1 Select F4	You'll copy the text "National Sales" from here to F12.
Click	(The Copy button is in the Clipboard group.) To copy the contents of the selected cell. A marquee appears, indicating that you've copied the cell data to the Clipboard.
2 Select F12	
Click	To paste the copied text. "National sales" now appears in F12, while also remaining in F4. Notice that the marquee is still visible; this indicates that you can paste another copy of the text in another location.
3 Copy A1	Select A1 and click the Copy button.
Select D1	This is the destination cell.
4 Click the bottom half of the **Paste** button	To display the paste options, which determine what is pasted in the destination.
Under Paste, point to	(The Paste button.) A preview of the pasted formatted text appears in cell D1.
Under Paste values, point to	A preview of the unformatted text is displayed in cell D1.
5 Under Other Paste Options, click	To paste only the formatting of A1 into D1, not the content. The text "Employee info" disappears from D1.
6 In D1, enter **2010**	The text appears with the same formatting as the text in A1.
7 Save the workbook	Click the Save button.

TIPS✓ *Tell students they can also press Ctrl+C.*

Objective 2.1.1.4

Objective 2.1.1.3

Objective 2.1.1.1

Drag-and-drop

Explanation

Drag-and-drop is a method of moving or copying data. *Dragging* is the act of pointing to a cell, holding down the mouse button, and then moving the pointer without releasing the mouse button. *Dropping* is releasing the mouse button after the pointer reaches the destination cell. (The term "dragging," however, often refers to the whole drag-and-drop procedure.)

Objective 2.1.3

To move the contents of a cell by using the drag-and-drop method:

1 Select the cell that contains the data you want to move.
2 Point to the border of the cell. The pointer changes to a four-headed arrow.
3 Drag the cell to where you want to move the data. As you drag, a cell outline shows where the data will go when you release the mouse button.
4 Release the mouse button when the pointer reaches the destination cell.

To copy a cell's contents to another cell:

1 Select the cell that contains the data you want to copy.
2 Point to the border of the cell until the pointer changes to a four-headed arrow.
3 Press and hold Ctrl. The pointer displays a plus sign (+), indicating that the selected data will be copied.
4 Drag to the destination cell, release the mouse button, and then release the Ctrl key.

Cut and paste vs. drag-and-drop

How you move and copy data between cells is a matter of preference. However, when the destination cell is not visible on the screen, cutting and pasting is usually most effective. If you have to scroll vertically or horizontally to get to the destination cell, use the Cut and Paste method. For short moves within the current view, however, it's often faster and easier to simply drag the formula to its destination cell and drop it there.

Do it!

Objective 2.1.3

A-3:   Moving and copying data by using drag-and-drop

Here's how	Here's why
1 Select D17	You'll move the contents of this cell to D19.
2 Point to the edge of the cell, as shown	 *Sales and Marketing* *Administration* *Acquisition* *Acquisition* The pointer changes to a four-headed arrow.
Press and hold the mouse button	
While holding down the mouse button, drag to D19	 *Sales and Marketing* *Administration* *Acquisition* *D19* *Acquisition* The boundary of D19 appears highlighted, and a ScreenTip provides the cell reference.
Release the mouse button	To drop the data in D19. D17 is now empty because the content was moved.
3 Point to the edge of D19	The pointer changes to a four-headed arrow.
Press and hold (CTRL)	 *Administration* *Sales and Marketing* *Acquisition* *Acquisition* *Administration* The pointer displays a plus sign, indicating that a copy will be made.
While holding (CTRL), drag to D17	 *Administration* *D17* *Sales and Marketing* *Acquisition* *Acquisition* *Administration*
Release the mouse button and then release (CTRL)	To drop the copied data. D17 now contains the data that's in D19, and D19 retains its data.
4 Save the workbook	

The Office Clipboard

Explanation

Microsoft Office applications include a special Clipboard, called the *Office Clipboard*, which expands the functionality of copy/paste and cut/paste. The Office Clipboard can hold multiple items—you're not limited to pasting the most recently cut or copied item. In addition, all items stored in the Office Clipboard are available to all open Microsoft Office applications.

Collect and Paste

You can use Collect and Paste to copy several items from any combination of Microsoft Office applications to a single location. For example, you might need to include content from a Microsoft Word document, a Web page, and a Microsoft PowerPoint presentation in a single worksheet. To do this, collect all the items in the Office Clipboard by switching to each source and copying the needed items. Then, you can switch to the worksheet and paste the items from the Office Clipboard, either separately or all at once.

The Clipboard task pane

You use the Clipboard task pane to view items on the Office Clipboard. You can copy up to 24 items to the Office Clipboard. When you close the Clipboard task pane, these items are not cleared; however, the Office Clipboard becomes inactive and the standard Clipboard is used instead to copy and paste items. The standard Windows Clipboard is limited to the most recently copied or cut item.

To open the Clipboard task pane, click the arrow button in the bottom-right corner of the Clipboard group. The following table describes the buttons in the Clipboard task pane.

Button	What it does
Paste All	Pastes multiple items simultaneously.
Clear All	Clears the Clipboard.
Options ▼	Contains options that control how the Office Clipboard is displayed.

Do it!

A-4:   Using the Clipboard task pane

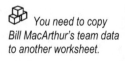 *You need to copy Bill MacArthur's team data to another worksheet.*

Here's how	Here's why
1 Click the arrow in the bottom-right corner of the Clipboard group, as shown	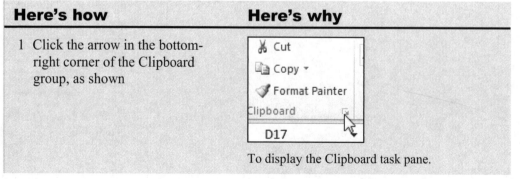
	To display the Clipboard task pane.

If the Clipboard is empty, the Clear All button will be disabled. Have students go right to Step 3.

Help students select the range, if necessary.

2 Click **Clear All**	(In the Clipboard task pane.) To clear the Clipboard.
3 Select the range A3:G3	(Drag from A3 to G3.) These cells contain the column headings. You'll copy them to the Clipboard.
Press CTRL + C	(Or click the Copy button in the Clipboard group.) To copy the contents of the range you selected to the Clipboard.
Observe the Clipboard pane	The items you just copied are displayed as plain text. You can use the Clipboard pane to quickly scan a list of options among several items stored on the Clipboard.
4 Copy the contents of A5:G9 to the Clipboard	These rows contain information about Bill MacArthur's team.
Observe the Clipboard pane	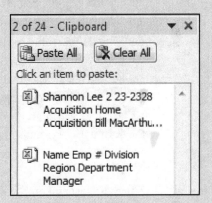 Both copied items are now listed in the Clipboard task pane.
5 Click the **File** tab and click **New**	
Verify that **Blank Workbook** is selected	
Click **Create**	(On the right side of the screen.) To create a new blank workbook.
6 In the Clipboard pane, click **Paste All**	Both copied items are pasted into the new workbook. You'll learn how to adjust the column widths later.
7 Save the workbook as **My Team** and close it	
8 Close the Clipboard pane	Click the X in the upper-right corner of the pane.
9 Save and close My Data	

Tell students that the text looks truncated because the data is too wide to fit in the columns. Students will learn how to adjust column widths later.

Topic B: Moving and copying formulas

This topic covers the following Microsoft Office Specialist objectives for exam 77-882: Excel 2010.

#	Objective
2.1	**Construct cell data**
	2.1.1 Use Paste Special
	2.1.1.10 Paste as link
2.2	**Apply AutoFill**
	2.2.1 Copy data

Moving formulas

Explanation

A formula can contain references, values, operators, or functions. The formula in a cell determines the value to be displayed. You move formulas the same way as any other data. When the same formula is needed in several locations, copy it to those locations instead of retyping it in each cell.

If you move a formula from one location to another, the calculation that was performed at the first location will be performed at the new location. Any references you used in the formula will remain the same.

Shortcut menus

For most screen components, you can use the right mouse button to display a shortcut menu. A *shortcut menu* provides a short list of commands related to the screen element you right-clicked. For example, when you right-click a cell, a shortcut menu is displayed containing several commands and options.

Do it!

B-1: Moving a formula

The files for this activity are in Student Data folder **Unit 3\Topic B**.

📦 *Students will enter a formula in the wrong column and then move it to the correct location.*

Here's how	Here's why
1 Open Formulas	
Save the workbook as **My Formulas**	
2 In H5, enter **=C5+D5+E5+F5**	You'll move this formula to column G.
3 Right-click H5	To display a shortcut menu.
Choose **Cut**	A marquee appears around the cell.
4 Right-click H6	To display a shortcut menu for that cell.
Click 📋	The formula is moved to H6. You realize that's not the right place for this formula. Because it provides the total of C5:F5, it should be placed in G5, in the Total column.
5 Select H6	If necessary.
Point to the cell border	↕ ↕ $23,442.00
	The pointer changes to a four-headed arrow.
Drag to G5	To move the formula to its proper location.
6 Save the workbook	

Point out that students are pasting the formula into the wrong cell temporarily to explore both methods of moving a formula.

Copying formulas

Explanation

You can copy and paste formulas to reuse them. Formulas are copied the same as any other data. Any references in the formula are adjusted to reflect the new location of the copied formula. (This is different from moving a formula, which retains its original cell references.)

Relative cell references

A *reference* identifies a cell or a range of cells in a worksheet; that is, it specifies a cell's location in a worksheet. For example, when you refer to a cell as B2, it means that the position of that specific cell is where column B intersects row 2.

By default, Excel uses *relative* cell references in formulas. When Excel checks the references in a formula you write, it sees those references in relation to the location of the formula.

Excel adjusts relative cell references when you copy a formula to a new location. For example, if you refer to cell C1 in a formula contained in D1, and you copy the formula to D2, the reference in the formula automatically changes to C2.

Exhibit 3-2 and Exhibit 3-3 illustrate this further. The formula in A3 is the sum of A1 and A2. If you copy this formula to B3, Excel automatically adjusts the cell references to correctly add B1 and B2, instead of merely duplicating the sum of A1 and A2.

A3		▾	f_x	=A1+A2
	A	B	C	D
1	10	20		
2	20	30		
3	30			
4				

Exhibit 3-2: A basic formula

B3		▾	f_x	=B1+B2	
	A	B	C	D	E
1	10	20			
2	20	30			
3	30	50			
4					

Exhibit 3-3: The copied formula pasted into B3 automatically adjusts

Do it!   **B-2:   Copying a formula**

Here's how	Here's why
1 Select G5	If necessary.
Review the formula	f_x =C5+D5+E5+F5
	(In the formula bar.) You'll copy this formula to G6. The references are all in row 5. These are relative references; Excel will adjust them when you copy the formula to a new location.
2 Copy the formula	Use any method you like.
3 Select G6	
Paste the formula	
Check the formula	f_x =C6+D6+E6+F6
	The references are now all in row 6.
4 Save the workbook	

Copying a formula with AutoFill

Explanation

Objective 2.2.1

You can use AutoFill to copy a formula to adjacent cells. Here's how:

1 Select the cell containing the formula you want to copy.

2 Point to the fill handle until the pointer changes to a + symbol.

3 Drag the fill handle over the adjacent cells to which you want to copy the formula.

+6.00	$5,956.00	$6,2
50.00	$5,700.00	$6,2
58.00	$5,858.00	$4

— Fill handle

Exhibit 3-4: The fill handle

Do it!

Objective 2.2.1

B-3: Using AutoFill to copy a formula

Here's how	Here's why
1 Select G6	(If necessary.) It contains the formula =C6+D6+E6+F6.
2 Point to the fill handle, as shown	$23,442.00 $24,755.00 The pointer changes to a plus sign (+). You can use the fill handle to copy this formula to adjacent cells.
3 Drag the fill handle to G7, as shown	$23,442.00 $24,755.00 As you drag, a shaded outline appears around the range you're filling with the copied data. The value appears in G7, and an Auto Fill Options button is displayed.
4 Click as shown	$24,755.00 $23,765.00 Auto Fill Options To display the shortcut menu for Auto Fill Options. Copy Cells is selected by default.
Click the Auto Fill Options button again	To close the shortcut menu.
5 Select G7	Excel adjusted the relative cell references so that the formula is now =C7+D7+E7+F7.
6 Save the workbook	

Pasting a link

Explanation

Objective 2.1.1.10

Once data has been copied and pasted, there is no connection between the original (or source) range and the destination range. You can maintain a connection, or link, between the source and destination ranges by using the Paste Link command. Then when the source data is changed, the data in the destination range will automatically update to reflect the changes.

To paste data with a link to the source:

1   Select the range containing the data to be copied.
2   Click Copy.
3   Select the destination range.
4   Right-click and choose Paste Special, and then click Paste Link. (You can also click the Paste Link button in the paste options.)

Do it!

Objective 2.1.1.10

Explain that this activity demonstrates the benefit of pasting a link.

B-4:   Using Paste Link

Here's how	Here's why
1 Select A4:A7	
Press CTRL + C	To copy the sales names.
2 Select A20	
Press CTRL + V	To paste the names in A20:A23.
3 Copy G4 and paste in B20	To copy the Total heading.
4 Copy G5:G7	(Select G5:G7 and click Copy.) You will copy the totals for each salesperson.
5 Select B21	To select the destination range.
Right-click and choose **Paste Special...**	To open the Paste Special dialog box.
6 Click **Paste Link**	The totals appear in the destination range.
Widen column B	If necessary.
7 Select B21	
Observe the formula bar	f_x =G5
	B21 contains a cell reference for Kendra's total sales and not the actual formula.
8 Edit C5 to be **2000**	When the formula in G5 recalculates, the value displayed in B21 automatically updates to reflect the change.
9 Update and close the workbook	

TIPS *Students can also click the Paste Link button in the paste options.*

Topic C: Absolute and relative references

This topic covers the following Microsoft Office Specialist objectives for exam 77-882: Excel 2010.

#	Objective
5.3	**Apply cell references**
	5.3.1 Relative and absolute references

This topic covers the following Microsoft Office Specialist objectives for exam 77-888: Excel Expert 2010.

#	Objective
2.1	**Audit formulas**
	2.1.5 Locate invalid formulas

Limitations of relative cell references

Explanation

Relative references are the default in Excel, and they make it simple for you to copy most formulas to several places. Sometimes, however, you won't want Excel to adjust references when you copy a formula. There will likely be times when you'll want to copy a formula but retain its original cell references. To address this situation, you can use absolute references or mixed references. First, you'll explore the limitations of relative cell references.

Invalid formulas

Expert objective 2.1.5

If a formula refers to a cell that should not change when you copy the formula, the copied formula will produce undesired results when you paste it, thus creating an invalid formula. Invalid formulas can be recognized by #VALUE! in the cell.

Undoing a mistake

If you make a mistake in Excel, it's easy to reverse. Simply click the Undo button on the Quick Access toolbar, or press Ctrl+Z. The Undo command reserves the most recent actions.

Do it!

C-1:   Observing the limitations of relative references

The files for this activity are in Student Data folder **Unit 3\Topic C**.

Here's how	Here's why
1 Open Bonus sales Save the workbook as **My Bonus sales**	
2 Observe H2	It contains the commission rate for bonus sales. You'll create formulas in column H to calculate actual commissions based on this rate.
3 In H5, enter **=G5*H2**	To calculate Kendra James's commission on bonus sales.
4 Select H5 Drag the fill handle to H7	You'll copy this formula to H6 and H7. Comm 937.68 To copy the formula down through the column.
Expert objective 2.1.5 5 Select H6	It displays $0.00 because the formula multiplied Pamela Carter's total in G6 by H3, which has no data. Excel adjusted this reference relative to the location of the new formula, resulting in an invalid formula.
6 Select H7	It displays an error value. In this case, the references have been adjusted such that the formula multiplies the sales total by the text "Comm" in H4. An error indicator appears in the top-left corner of the cell.
7 Click ↰	(The Undo button is on the Quick Access toolbar.) To undo your last action.
8 Save the workbook	

TIPS ✔ *Students can also press Ctrl+Z to undo an action.*

Absolute references

Explanation

Objective 5.3.1

When you don't want a reference to change when you copy it, you can use an *absolute reference*. To make a reference absolute, insert a dollar sign in front of both the column letter and the row number of the reference. For example, to create an absolute reference to cell A1, you would enter A1 in a formula. When you copy an absolute reference to another location, Excel does not adjust the reference.

You can enter a cell reference and then press F4 to make that reference absolute. This is often faster and easier than manually entering multiple dollar signs in a formula.

Mixed references

You can create *mixed references* by placing a dollar sign in front of only the column letter or only the row number. When you copy the formula, the relative part of the reference will adjust relative to the new location, but the absolute part will not. You can cycle through the reference possibilities by pressing F4 when you're entering a reference.

Do it!

Objective 5.3.1

C-2:   Applying absolute references

Here's how	Here's why
1 Select H5	(If necessary.) You'll adjust the reference to the commission rate to make it absolute.
2 Place the insertion point in the formula bar as shown	✗ ✓ *fx* =G5*H2
Press F4	✗ ✓ *fx* =G5*H2 To change the cell reference to H2, making it an absolute reference.
Press ↵ ENTER	To enter the formula.
3 Select H5	
Copy the formula to H6 and H7	Use the fill handle.
4 Select H6	*fx* =G6*H2 H6 now displays the correct value. In the formula, the first reference was adjusted relative to the formula's location. However, the absolute reference, H2, remained unchanged.
5 Verify that the formula in H7 uses an absolute reference	
6 Save and close the workbook	

Students can also enter the $ characters directly in a cell.

Topic D: Inserting and deleting ranges, rows, and columns

Explanation   A row, column, or range of cells can be inserted in or deleted from a workbook.

Inserting cells

To insert a range of cells in a worksheet:

1   Select the range where you want to insert the cells. To select a range, click the first cell you want to select, and drag to the last cell you want to select. (Do not use the fill handle while dragging.)

2   In the Cells group of the Home tab, click Insert to display a menu.

3   Choose Insert Cells to open the Insert dialog box.

4   Specify whether you want to shift cells or insert an entire row or column, and click OK.

D-1:   Inserting a range of cells

The files for this activity are in Student Data folder **Unit 3\Topic D**.

Here's how	Here's why
1 Open Sales totals	
Save the workbook as **My Sales totals**	
2 Select A6:H6	You'll insert a range of cells to store data for a new sales representative.
3 On the Home tab, in the Cells group, click as shown	
	To display the Insert menu.
Choose **Insert Cells...**	To open the Insert dialog box. When you insert cells, you need to specify which way to shift the selected cells. "Shift cells down" is selected by default.
Click **OK**	To insert the range and shift the cells down.
4 In row 6, enter the following data	

6	Alan Monder		22	$7,500.00	$6,550.00	$5,700.00	$6,200.00

5 Select G5:H5	You'll fill these formulas down to complete Alan Monder's data.
Drag the fill handle down to H6	
	To copy the total and commission formulas to Alan Monder's row.
6 Save the workbook	

Depending on the resolution of students' screens, the button might look different from that shown. Make sure students click the arrow next to or below the Insert button.

Tell students to enter only the values. Excel will automatically format them with dollar signs and decimal points.

Inserting rows and columns

Explanation

To insert a row or column:

1   Select the row or column where you want to insert a new row or column. (You can click the column and row heading buttons to select entire columns and rows.)

2   Do either of the following:

- Right-click the selected area to display a shortcut menu, and choose Insert.
- Click Insert (in the Cells group), and then choose Insert Sheet Rows or Insert Sheet Columns.

When you insert a row or column, you don't have to specify where to shift cells. The new row will be inserted above the selected row, and a new column will be inserted to the left of the selected column.

If you want to insert multiple rows or columns simultaneously, select the number of rows or columns that equal the number of rows or columns you want to insert.

Do it!

D-2:   Inserting rows

Here's how	Here's why
1 Drag over the numbered labels for rows 5–8, as shown	4 Name 5 Kendra James 6 Alan Monder 7 Pamela Carter ⦈ Julie George To select the entire rows. You'll insert four rows simultaneously.
2 Right-click the selection	To display a shortcut menu.
Choose **Insert**	To insert four rows above the four selected rows.
Click ↰	To undo the last action.
3 Select row 8	Click the row heading for row 8.
4 Right-click the selection and choose **Insert**	To insert a row above the selected row. When you insert an entire row or column, you don't need to specify how to shift the remaining cells.
5 In row 8, enter the following data	
8 Audrey Cress 27 $7,500.00 $4,500.00 $5,200.00 $7,500.00	
6 Copy the formulas from G7:H7 to G8:H8	To complete the new employee data.
7 Save the workbook	

Deleting cell ranges

Explanation

To delete a range of cells:

1 Select the range you want to delete.
2 In the Cells group, click Delete. You can also right-click the selection and choose Delete from the shortcut menu.
3 Specify where to shift the adjacent cells.
4 Click OK.

If you're deleting an entire row or column, you don't need to specify where to shift cells.

Do it!

D-3: Deleting a range of cells

Pamela Carter has left the company, so students will delete her data from the worksheet.

Here's how	Here's why
1 Select A7:H7	A7:H7 contains the data for Pamela Carter.
2 Right-click the selection and choose **Delete...**	To open the Delete dialog box. "Shift cells up" is selected by default.
Click **OK**	To delete the selected range and shift the remaining cells up.
3 Undo the deletion	You'll perform the last action again, this time deleting the entire row.
4 Select row 7	Click the row-heading button (7).
Right-click the selection and choose **Delete**	To delete the selected row. When you delete an entire row or column, you are not prompted to specify where to shift the remaining cells.
5 Save and close the workbook	

Unit summary: Modifying a worksheet

Topic A   In this topic, you learned how to **move and copy data** in a worksheet. You learned that you can do this by using the Cut, Copy, and Paste buttons in the Clipboard group. You also learned how to move and copy data by using drag-and-drop and the Clipboard. You learned that you can use the **Office Clipboard** to copy and paste multiple items simultaneously.

Topic B   In this topic, you learned how to move and copy **formulas**, and you learned about **relative cell references**. You also learned how to use AutoFill to copy data to adjacent cells.

Topic C   In this topic, you learned about the limitations of relative references in certain circumstances. You then learned how to apply **absolute references**.

Topic D   In this topic, you learned how to insert and delete **ranges** and entire rows and columns.

Independent practice activity

In this activity, you'll insert a row and copy and delete data. Then you'll create a formula and copy it, using both relative and absolute references.

The files for this activity are in Student Data folder **Unit 3\Unit summary**.

1 Open Southern sales and save it as **My Southern sales**.

2 Insert a row above row 10.

3 Copy the data for 2010 sales to the new row 10. (*Hint:* Copy A15:E15.)

4 Delete the row containing the data for sales in the year 2005.

5 In cell F5, enter a formula to calculate the total sales for 2006.

6 Copy the yearly total formula to F6:F9.

7 In F10, enter a formula that will calculate the total sales for the five-year period. Use absolute references so that you can copy the formula without changing the references later.

8 Copy the formula in F10 to A19.

9 Change the value in B5 to 11000.

10 Verify the resulting change in values in A19 and C19, and compare your work with Exhibit 3-5.

11 Save and close the workbook.

▲	A	B	C	D	E	F	G
1		**Outlander Spices**					
2	**Yearly bonus sales for the northern region (all figures in $)**						
3							
4	Year	Qtr1	Qtr2	Qtr3	Qtr4	Total	
5	2006	11000	15478	18756	17563	62797	
6	2007	17895	19872	19653	19845	77265	
7	2008	22156	14235	15698	21036	73125	
8	2009	20789	12458	13698	18654	65599	
9	2010	9109	14825	16682	19295	59911	
10			Total of last five years			338697	
11							
12	**Sales for 2010**						
13	Year	Qtr1	Qtr2	Qtr3	Qtr4		
14	2010	9109	14825	16682	19295		
15							
16	**Profit earned in last five years**						
17							
18	Total of last five years	% Profit	Profit amount				
19	338697	20	67739.4				

Exhibit 3-5: The completed worksheet

Review questions

1 What is meant by the term "relative cell reference?"

The cell address is interpreted in relation to the location of the formula. Excel adjusts the relative cell references when you copy a formula to a new location.

2 Describe one limitation of a relative reference.

If a formula refers to a specific cell that should not change when you copy the formula, the formula containing a relative reference will produce an incorrect result when you copy it.

3 How do you designate a reference as an absolute reference?

Place a dollar sign in front of both the column letter and the row number.

4 How can you avoid having to enter multiple dollar signs when creating absolute references?

Type the cell reference and then press F4 to make the cell reference absolute. Repeat this for each cell reference in the formula.

5 How can you create a mixed reference?

Place a dollar sign in front of only the column letter or only the row number in a cell reference. When you copy the formula, the relative part of the reference will adjust relative to the new location, but the absolute part will not.

Unit 4

Using functions

Unit time: 45 minutes

Complete this unit, and you'll know how to:

A Apply the SUM function to calculate the sum of values.

B Use AutoSum to enter SUM functions.

C Use the AVERAGE, MIN, MAX, COUNT, and COUNTA functions to find average, minimum, and maximum values and the count of cells in a range.

Topic A: Entering functions

This topic covers the following Microsoft Office Specialist objectives for exam 77-882: Excel 2010.

#	Objective
5.6	**Apply cell ranges in formulas**
	5.6.1 Enter a cell range definition in the formula bar
	5.6.2 Define a cell range

This topic covers the following Microsoft Office Specialist objectives for exam 77-888: Excel Expert 2010.

#	Objective
2.4	**Apply functions in formulas**
	2.4.1 Find and correct errors in functions

The structure of functions

Explanation

Performing calculations on each value in a range of cells can be complicated and time-consuming. For example, if you have a range of 20 cells, a formula that adds the value in each cell will be long. To simplify such long or complex tasks, use Excel functions. If you insert cells within the range used in a function, the function will automatically adjust to include the new cells.

A *function* is a predefined formula that performs a specific calculation or other action on numbers or text. You specify the values on which the function performs the calculations. Functions have the following structure, or syntax:

    =FUNCTIONNAME(ARGUMENT1,ARGUMENT2,...)

Like formulas, functions begin with an equal sign. Following that is the name of the function and then a set of parentheses enclosing the input values for the function.

Arguments are the input values of a function. Arguments can be numbers, text, cell addresses, ranges, or other functions.

The SUM function

One of the most commonly used functions is *SUM*, which calculates the total of all of the values listed in its arguments. It has the following structure:

    =SUM(number1,number2,...)

For example, the function =SUM(2, 3) calculates the sum of 2 and 3, returning the value 5. Consider the data in Exhibit 4-1 and the functions in the table that follows.

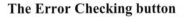

	A
1	10
2	20
3	30
4	40

Exhibit 4-1: Sample data

Function	Result
=SUM(A1, A2)	30
=SUM(A1, A4)	50
=SUM(A2,100)	120

Contiguous range references

Objective 5.6.2

To enter a contiguous range of cells in a formula or function, type the first cell in the range, followed by a colon (:) and the last cell in the range. For example, in Exhibit 4-1, the sum of cells A1, A2, A3, and A4 is written as:

```
=SUM(A1:A4)
```

The Error Checking button

Expert objective 2.4.1

When Excel suspects that there might be an error in a cell, it warns you by displaying a green triangle, called the *error indicator*, in the top-left corner of the cell. When you select the cell, the Error Checking button appears; you can click it to display a menu of actions you can perform on the formula. You can use this menu to resolve the error or ignore it, or you can use one of the error-checking options.

Syntax errors

A *syntax error* occurs when a formula or function is entered in the wrong format or is missing some required punctuation. When a function is entered incorrectly, Excel attempts to diagnose the error. If it appears to be a syntax error, Excel will suggest a solution. For example, say you enter a function to sum cells A1 through A4 as follows:

```
=SUM(A1;A4)
```

Because a semicolon (;) was entered instead of a colon (:), an error message appears, as shown in Exhibit 4-2.

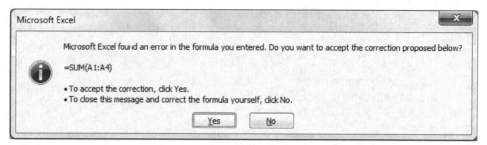

Exhibit 4-2: An Excel message box suggesting a solution for a simple syntax error

Do it!

A-1: Entering a SUM function

The files for this activity are in Student Data folder **Unit 4\Topic A**.

Here's how	Here's why
1 Open Northern sales Save the workbook as **My Northern sales**	
2 Select G5	You'll enter a SUM function here to calculate Kendra James's sales total for the year.
3 Type **=**	All formulas, including functions, begin with the equal sign (=).
Type **SUM(**	To enter the name of the function and an opening parenthesis. A function argument ScreenTip appears when you type the open parenthesis.
Type **C5:F5**	To enter a range reference as an argument for the function. The function will calculate the sum of the values in C5, D5, E5, and F5.
Type **)**	f_x =SUM(C5:F5) The closing parenthesis completes the function.
4 Press (↵ ENTER)	To enter the function, returning the value 23442.
5 Select G5	An error indicator appears in the upper-left corner of the cell, and the Error Checking button appears next to the cell.
6 Point to the Error Checking button, as shown below	A long ScreenTip appears, describing the possible error in the cell formula.

TIPS   You can use uppercase or lowercase text in formulas. Case does not matter.

Objective 5.6.2

Expert objective 2.4.1

Point out that just because Excel suspects there might be an error, this doesn't mean there is one.

◈ ▾	23442
623	26121
786	The formula in this cell refers to a range that has additional numbers adjacent to it.
343	

7 Click the Error Checking button

To display a menu.

Observe the menu

⚠ ▾	23442	
Formula Omits Adjacent Cells		
Update Formula to Include Cells		
Help on this error		
Ignore Error		
Edit in Formula Bar		
Error Checking Options...		

The Formula Omits Adjacent Cells error is highlighted because the function doesn't include the value in the Employee number column. This is not an error; that number should not be included in the sum.

Choose **Ignore Error**

To accept the formula as it is and hide the error indicator.

8 Edit F5 to read **1000**

Observe G5

The sum changed from 23442 to 16158. Functions are automatically updated when the values in their ranges are changed.

Undo the change

Click the Undo button on the Quick Access toolbar or press Ctrl+Z.

Expert objective 2.4.1

9 Select G6

You'll enter a SUM function that contains a syntax error.

Type **=SUM C6:F6**

To enter the function without its required parentheses.

Press (↵ ENTER)

A message box appears, reporting an error in the function and proposing a correction.

Tell students that the error indicator will still appear in the cell for the same reason as before.

Click **Yes**

To accept the proposed correction. Excel adds the missing parentheses to the function.

10 Hide the error indicator in the cell

Select G6, click the Error Checking button, and choose Ignore Error.

11 Save the workbook

Using the mouse to enter range references

Explanation

You can use the mouse to enter a range reference in a formula or function. To do so:

1 Type the equal sign, the function name, and the opening parenthesis for the function.

2 Drag to select a range for the reference.

3 Type the closing parenthesis and press Enter. (Or you can first enter more arguments and type a comma to separate each argument.)

Do it!

A-2: Using the mouse to enter a function argument

Here's how	Here's why
1 Select G7	You'll use the SUM function to calculate the sales total for Audrey Kress.
2 Type **=SUM(**	You'll use the mouse to enter the argument for this function. A ScreenTip appears below the cell.

Drag from C7 to F7, as shown

Emp #	Qtr1	Qtr2	Qtr3	Qtr4	Total
16	6354	4846	3958	8284	23442
22	7546	6574	5767	6234	26121
27	7635	4765	5256	⊕ 7865	=sum(C7:F7

	As you drag, the reference for the selected range appears in the function. A marquee surrounds the selected range.
Press (↵ ENTER)	Excel automatically inserts the closing parenthesis and enters the function.
Ignore the error indicator in G7	Again, the employee number in B7 is correctly omitted from the sum.

3 Save the workbook

Entering functions in the formula bar

Explanation

Objective 5.6.1

You can enter text, numbers, and formulas directly in the formula bar. When the formula bar is activated, Cancel and Enter buttons appear to the left of it.

To enter a function in the formula bar:

1 Click the formula bar to activate it.
2 Type = and then the function name, such as SUM. For example, =SUM.
3 Type the cell range enclosed in parentheses.
4 Click Enter.

Do it!

Objective 5.6.1

A-3:   Entering a function in the formula bar

Here's how	Here's why
1 Select G8	
2 Click the formula bar	To activate it. A Cancel button and an Enter button appear.
3 Type **=SUM(C8:F8)**	✗ ✓ *fx* =SUM(C8:F8) To calculate the quarterly sales for Julie George.
4 Click ✓	To enter the formula.
5 Ignore the error indicator in G8	
6 Save the workbook	

Inserting functions

Explanation

You don't need to memorize all the available functions and the arguments required for each function. Instead, you can use the Insert Function dialog box, which lists all available functions. When you choose a function, Excel prompts you for both required and optional arguments.

To insert a function:

1 Select the cell where you want to enter the function.
2 Click the Insert Function button on the formula bar to open the Insert Function dialog box.
3 Select a function category and a function, and click OK. Excel opens the Function Arguments dialog box that's specific to the chosen function (as shown in Exhibit 4-3).
4 In the argument boxes, enter arguments for the function. You can use the Collapse buttons (to the right of the text boxes) to minimize the dialog box temporarily, and then select cells or ranges by using the mouse.
5 Click OK.

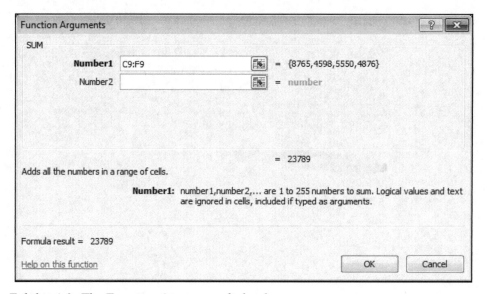

Exhibit 4-3: The Function Arguments dialog box

Do it!

A-4:   Inserting a function

Here's how	Here's why
1 Select G9	You'll enter a SUM function here by using the Insert Function dialog box.
2 Click f_x	(The Insert Function button is on the formula bar.) To open the Insert Function dialog box. You'll choose a function category and a function.
3 Observe the dialog box	You can type a function in the "Search for a function" box, or select a category to view all available functions in that category. The SUM function is already selected because Most Recently Used is the default category.
Click **OK**	To open the Function Arguments dialog box.
4 Click as shown	**Number1** G5:G8 Number2
	To collapse the dialog box. Now you can use the mouse to enter the argument for the function.
Select C9:F9	To select the range as the argument for the SUM function.
Press ← ENTER	To enter the argument and expand the dialog box again. The formula result is displayed at the bottom of the dialog box.
5 Click **OK**	To insert the function and close the dialog box.
Save and close the workbook	

Topic B: AutoSum

Explanation

Entering references for a long range in a sum formula can be a tedious task prone to error. Excel's AutoSum feature automatically inserts the Sum formula and arguments for a function.

Applying AutoSum

When you select a cell and click the AutoSum button, Excel guesses the range of values you want to use as the argument, as shown in Exhibit 4-4 and Exhibit 4-5. For example, if you use the button at the bottom of a column of numbers, Excel assumes that the cells above the current cell should be used as the function argument. However, this guess is not always what you want. You can either accept this argument or enter your own.

Qtr1	Qtr2	Qtr3
6354	4846	3958
7546	6574	5767
7635	4765	5256
9595	5859	4879
8765	4598	5550
=SUM(C5:C9)		
SUM(**number1**, [number2], ...)		

Exhibit 4-4: The AutoSum function guesses which range of data to use

Emp #	Qtr1	Qtr2	Qtr3	Qtr4	Total	
16	6354	4846	3958	8284	=SUM(B5:F5)	
22	7546	6574	5767	6234	SUM(**number1**, [number2], ...)	
20	9595	5859	4879	3432	23765	

Exhibit 4-5: The guess is not always correct

Using AutoSum to enter several functions

AutoSum can also enter SUM functions at several locations simultaneously. For example, if you want to enter totals at the bottom of several columns of values, select all of the cells that should contain the SUM function and then click the AutoSum button. Although this process is simple and fast, you need to ensure that the cells you select for inserting the functions are correct.

Do it!   **B-1:   Using AutoSum**

The files for this activity are in Student Data folder **Unit 4\Topic B**.

Here's how	Here's why
1 Open Quarterly sales	
Save the workbook as **My Quarterly sales**	
2 Select C10	You'll enter a SUM function to calculate the Qtr1 total.
In the Editing group, click as shown	

At lower resolutions or on smaller screens, the icon might look different. Help students use the correct command, if necessary.

The AutoSum button displays a menu that includes several common functions.

3 Choose **SUM**	

To automatically create a SUM function.

Observe the formula bar and the highlighted cells in the worksheet	=SUM(C5:C9)

The argument for the function is C5:C9.

TIPS
Students can also click Enter in the formula bar.

Press ⏎ ENTER	To enter the function.
4 Select D10:G10	To specify a range of cells that will contain the formula.
5 Click Σ	To enter SUM functions in all of the selected cells.
6 Save and close the workbook	

Topic C: Other common functions

This topic covers the following Microsoft Office Specialist objectives for exam 77-882: Excel 2010.

#	Objective
2.1	**Construct cell data**
	2.1.1 Use Paste Special
	2.1.1.2 Formulas

This topic covers the following Microsoft Office Specialist objectives for exam 77-888: Excel Expert 2010.

#	Objective
2.4	**Apply functions in formulas**
	2.4.3 Use statistical functions

Statistical functions

Explanation

Excel provides hundreds of functions, from simple to complex. The functions list includes frequently used functions such as AVERAGE, MIN, MAX, COUNT, and COUNTA.

The AVERAGE function

Expert objective 2.4.3

The *AVERAGE* function calculates the arithmetic mean of a list of values. The function has the following syntax:

```
=AVERAGE(number1,number2,...)
```

In this function, the arguments *number1* and *number2* specify the values to be used in the calculation. Commas separate each argument. The average is determined by summing the values in the arguments and then dividing that sum by the number of values. Excel does not include blank cells when calculating the average. If the ranges you specify have no values in them, AVERAGE returns an error.

Using the AutoSum button to enter other functions

You already know how to use the AutoSum button to quickly apply the SUM function. You can also use this button to enter other functions, such as AVERAGE, MIN, MAX, and COUNT. To do so, click the arrow on the AutoSum button and select the desired function. Excel automatically specifies the range of values to be used as the function's arguments. You can either accept these arguments or enter your own.

Pasting only formulas

Objective 2.1.1.2

When you paste the copied data, the Paste Options button appears next to the destination cell. Click this button or press the Ctrl key to display the paste options, as shown in Exhibit 4-6. Click the Formulas button to paste only the formula.

Exhibit 4-6: The Paste Options shortcut menu

Do it!

C-1: Using AVERAGE

The files for this activity are in Student Data folder **Unit 4\Topic C**.

Expert objective 2.4.3

Here's how	Here's why
1 Open Sales data	
Save the workbook as **My Sales data**	
2 Select C12	You'll enter a function here to calculate the average of the bonus sales figures for Qtr1.

Remind students that they can use lowercase or uppercase letters.

3 Type **=av**

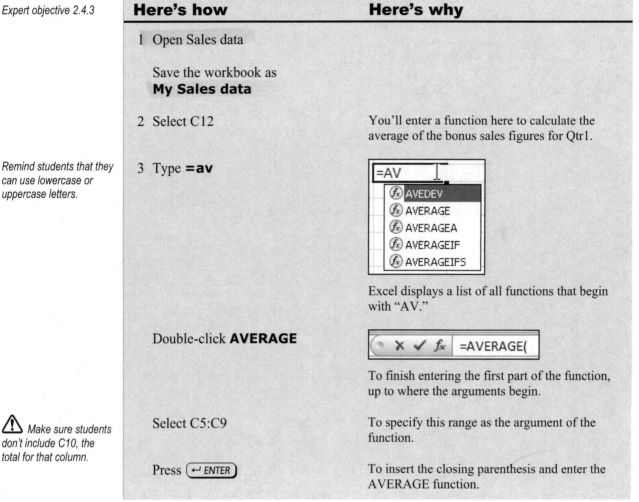

Excel displays a list of all functions that begin with "AV."

Double-click **AVERAGE**

To finish entering the first part of the function, up to where the arguments begin.

⚠ *Make sure students don't include C10, the total for that column.*

Select C5:C9

To specify this range as the argument of the function.

Press (↵ ENTER)

To insert the closing parenthesis and enter the AVERAGE function.

Again, the button might look different depending on the resolution and screen size.

4 Select D12

You'll calculate the average for Qtr2 sales.

In the Editing group, click as shown

To display a menu of functions.

Choose **Average**

Excel automatically takes C12 as the argument for the function because it's the only adjacent value. This is not the correct selection.

Select D5:D9

To specify this range as the argument of the function. A marquee appears around D5:D9.

Press ↵ ENTER

To enter the function. The average of the Qtr2 sales is displayed in D12.

Objective 2.1.1.2

5 Copy the function in D12 and paste it into E12

Use Ctrl+C to copy and Ctrl+V to paste.

Display the paste options and click *fx*

Click the Paste Options button or press Ctrl.

6 Copy the function in E12 to F12

Use any method you like.

7 Save the workbook

The MIN function

Explanation

Expert objective 2.4.3

The *MIN* function returns the smallest number from a list of values. This function has the following syntax:

```
=MIN(number1,number2,...)
```

Arguments for this function can include numbers, empty cells, logical values, or text representations of numbers (such as dates). Error values or text that can't be translated into numbers will produce an error.

Do it!

Expert objective 2.4.3

C-2: Using MIN

Here's how	Here's why
1 Select C13	You'll enter a function here to return the lowest Qtr1 value.
2 Type **=M**	To display a list of functions that begin with the letter M.
Double-click **MIN**	The MIN function returns the lowest value (the minimum) in the list of values specified as its argument.
Select C5:C9 and press (↵ ENTER)	To specify this range as the argument of the function.
3 Copy the formula in C13 to D13:F13	
4 Save the workbook	

The MAX function

Explanation

Expert objective 2.4.3

The *MAX* function returns the largest number in a list of values and has the following syntax:

```
=MAX(number1,number2,...)
```

Exhibit 4-7 shows the results of the MAX function for each quarter.

| Outlander Spices | | | | | | |
| Bonus sales for the northern region | | | | | | |
Name	Emp #	Qtr1	Qtr2	Qtr3	Qtr4	Total
Kendra James	16	6354	4846	3958	8284	23442
Alan Monder	22	7546	6574	5767	6234	26121
Audrey Kress	27	7635	4765	5256	7865	25521
Julie George	29	9595	5859	4879	3432	23765
James Overmire	42	8765	4598	5550	4876	23789
Totals		39895	26642	25410	30691	122638
Average		7979	5328.4	5082	6138.2	
Minimum		6354	4598	3958	3432	
Maximum		9595	6574	5767	8284	

Exhibit 4-7: Average, minimum, and maximum values

Do it!

Expert objective 2.4.3

C-3:   Using MAX

Here's how	Here's why
1 Select C14	You'll enter a function that will return the largest Qtr1 value.
2 Enter the first part of the **MAX** function	(Type =M and then double-click MAX in the list.) MAX is the function that returns the largest value (the maximum) in a list of values.
Select C5:C9 and press (↵ ENTER)	
3 Copy the formula in C14 to D14:F14	Compare your work to Exhibit 4-7.
4 Save the workbook	

The COUNT and COUNTA functions

Explanation

You can use the COUNT function to determine how many cells in a range contain numeric values. The COUNT function will recognize only cells that contain numbers; it will not count any cells that are blank or that contain text.

Expert objective 2.4.3

The syntax for COUNT is:

```
=COUNT(value1, value2,...)
```

The COUNTA function counts not only the number of cells that contain numbers, but also the number of cells containing text. COUNTA will not, however, include blank cells in the count. The syntax for the COUNTA function is:

```
=COUNTA(value1, value2,...)
```

Do it!

C-4: Using COUNT and COUNTA

Expert objective 2.4.3

Here's how	Here's why
1 Select C16	You'll determine the total number of Quarterly sales figures for the year.
2 Enter the first part of the COUNT function	To begin the formula.
Select C4:F9 and press ⏎ ENTER	To complete the formula and return the result. Note that even though you included C4:F4 in the range, those cells were not counted toward the total because they don't contain numeric values.
3 Select C17	You'll use COUNTA to count the number of Northern Region employees involved in the quarterly sales.
4 Enter the first part of the COUNTA function	
Select A5:A9 and press ⏎ ENTER	To complete the formula and return the result. COUNTA counts all non-empty cells.
5 Save and close the workbook	

Unit summary: Using functions

Topic A
In this topic, you learned that **functions** are predefined formulas you can use to perform calculations. You learned that all functions consist of an equal sign, the name of the function, and **arguments** enclosed in parentheses. You learned how to use the **SUM function** to add a list of values.

Topic B
In this topic, you learned how to use the **AutoSum** button. You learned that you can use AutoSum to enter a SUM function quickly, either in a single cell or in a range of cells.

Topic C
In this topic, you learned how to apply other **commonly used functions**, including AVERAGE, which calculates the average of a list of values, MIN, which calculates the lowest value in a list, and MAX, which calculates the highest value in a list. You also used COUNT and COUNTA to determine the number of cells in a selection.

Independent practice activity

In this activity, you'll enter functions to display the sum, average, minimum, and maximum of values. You'll also use the COUNT function.

The files for this activity are in Student Data folder **Unit 4\Unit summary**.

1 Open Softball and save it as **My Softball**. This workbook contains home-run statistics for the Outlander company softball team.

2 In B21, enter a function to calculate Bill MacArthur's total number of home runs.

3 In B22, enter a function to calculate Bill's average number of home runs per year.

4 In B23, enter a function to calculate his lowest number of home runs in a year.

5 In B24, enter a function to calculate Bill's highest number of home runs in a year.

6 In B25, enter a function to count the number of years Bill has been hitting home runs.

7 In G6, enter a formula to calculate how many home runs Bill needs to hit to tie Michael Lee's record. (*Hint:* This will be the difference between the values in cells G5 and B21. For example, the difference between the values in B10 and B15 would be written as =B10-B15.)

8 Compare your work to Exhibit 4-8.

9 Save and close the workbook.

	A	B	C	D	E	F	G	H
1	Outlander company softball team							
2	Home runs by Bill MacArthur by year							
3								
4	Year	Home runs						
5	1996	3			Michael Lee's record total:		175	
6	1997	8			HR MacArthur needs to tie:		22	
7	1998	16						
8	1999	10						
9	2000	7						
10	2001	2						
11	2002	14						
12	2003	9						
13	2004	9						
14	2005	19						
15	2006	18						
16	2007	12						
17	2008	10						
18	2009	7						
19	2010	9						
20								
21	Total	153						
22	Average	10.2						
23	Low	2						
24	High	19						
25	# of Years	15						
26								

Exhibit 4-8: The completed workbook

Review questions

1 What is a function?

   A predefined formula that performs a specific type of calculation.

2 True or false? When an error indicator appears in a cell, it means the cell contains an error.

   False. An error indicator (a green triangle that appears in the top-left corner of the cell) indicates that there might be an error so that you can check it and either ignore it or fix it.

3 What is the syntax for the SUM function?

   =SUM(number1,number2,...)

4 Which function is used to calculate the arithmetic mean of a list of values?

   The AVERAGE function

5 If your worksheet contains total sales figures for each of your salespeople, which function could you use to find the salesperson with the highest sales?

   The MAX function

6 Which function would you use to count the total number of sales transactions in a given time period?

   The COUNT function

Unit 5
Formatting

Unit time: 60 minutes

Complete this unit, and you'll know how to:

A Apply text formatting.

B Customize column widths, row heights, and alignment, and apply color and border formatting.

C Format values as currency, percentages, and ordinary numbers.

D Apply conditional formatting based on specific criteria.

E Copy formatting, apply cell styles and table styles, and use Find and Replace to update the formatting for specific content.

Topic A: Text formatting

Explanation   You can format text and values by changing the font, font size, style, and color. You can format all the text in an active cell or only a selected portion of it. You can also select multiple cells and apply formatting to all of them at once.

The Font group

The fastest way to apply formatting is to use the commands in the Font group, shown in Exhibit 5-1. This group (on the Home tab) provides tools for applying commonly used formats, such as boldface, italics, text color, background color, and borders.

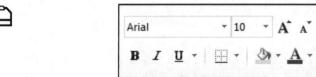

This Dialog Box Launcher opens the Format Cells dialog box, with the Font tab active

Exhibit 5-1: Formatting options in the Font group

The following table lists the buttons in the Font group.

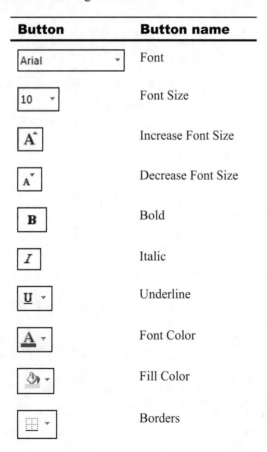

Button	Button name
Arial	Font
10	Font Size
A˄	Increase Font Size
A˅	Decrease Font Size
B	Bold
I	Italic
U	Underline
A	Font Color
(fill)	Fill Color
(border)	Borders

To format cells by using the Font group, select the cell or range you want to format and then click the formatting button you want. You can select a font and font size from the drop-down lists.

Do it!

A-1: Formatting text

The files for this activity are in Student Data folder **Unit 5\Topic A**.

Here's how	Here's why
1 Open Regional sales	The data in this workbook has no formatting.
2 Save the workbook as **My Regional sales**	
3 Select A6:B6	You'll make these headings stand out by changing their formatting.
In the Font group, click **B**	To make the headings in A6:B6 bold.
4 Select C6:F6	To select the heading titles for the quarterly sales figures.
Click *I*	(In the Font group.) To make the Qtr headings italic.
5 Select A1	You'll make the title text larger and change the font.
Click the Font Size arrow, as shown	10 ▾ To display a list of font sizes.
Select **16**	To increase the size of the text to 16 points.
6 Click as shown	Arial 16 **B** *I* <u>U</u> ▾ ▾ To display the Font list.
Move the pointer down through the list of fonts, while observing the text in A1	Because of the Live Preview feature, you can see how the selected text changes to indicate how it would look in each font.
Select **Arial Black**	
7 Make A2 italic	Select the cell and click the Italic button.
8 Save the workbook	

Tell students that font size is measured in points. There are 72 points in an inch. The default font size in Excel is 10 points.

Point out that this list uses Live Preview. When you point to a font size, the text in the selected cell appears in that size.

The Font list also uses Live Preview.

Formatting non-contiguous ranges

Explanation

You can quickly apply formatting to cells that are not adjacent to each other. For example, you might want to apply a specific format to cells A1 and B4 and the range C6:D7. To do this in one step, you can select them as a *non-contiguous range*—a range of cells located in non-adjacent areas of the worksheet.

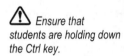

To select a non-contiguous range, select the first cell or range; then hold down the Ctrl key and select other cells or ranges you want to include. You can then format this range as you would format any other selection.

Do it!

A-2:   Formatting a non-contiguous range

Here's how	Here's why
1 Select G4	To select the first of the three non-contiguous areas you'll format. You'll apply bold formatting to G4, A11, and G6:H6 in a single step.
Press and hold (CTRL)	
Select A11	To add A11 to the selection.
Select G6:H6	To add this range to the selection.
Release (CTRL)	
2 Click **B**	To apply bold formatting to the selected non-contiguous range.
Deselect the range	Click any cell.
3 Save the workbook	

⚠ *Ensure that students are holding down the Ctrl key.*

The Format Cells dialog box

Explanation

The Format Cells dialog box provides several formatting options. With the Font tab (shown in Exhibit 5-2), you can set the font, style, size, and other options.

Exhibit 5-2: The Font tab in the Format Cells dialog box

To use the Format Cells dialog box to format cells:

1 Select the cell or range you want to format.

2 Right-click the selection and choose Format Cells to open the Format Cells dialog box.

3 If necessary, click the Font tab.

4 Apply the desired formatting options. You can see what the formatted cells will look like in the Preview box. Then click OK.

Do it!   **A-3:**   **Using the Format Cells dialog box to format text**

Here's how	Here's why
1 Select A1	You'll change the font and size of the worksheet title.
2 Right-click the selection	To display a shortcut menu.
Choose **Format Cells...**	To open the Format Cells dialog box.
Click the **Font** tab	If necessary.
3 From the Font list, select **Times New Roman**	Scroll down the Font list.
From the Font style list, select **Bold Italic**	
From the Size list, select **18**	
4 Observe the Preview box	The Preview box shows how the text will look with the selected formatting.
5 Click **OK**	To apply the formatting to the cell.
6 Select A2	
7 Open the Format Cells dialog box	
From the Font list, select **Times New Roman**	
From the Size list, select **12**, and then click **OK**	*Outlander Spices* Bonus sales for the northern region
8 Save and close the workbook	

Topic B: Row and column formatting

This topic covers the following Microsoft Office Specialist objectives for exam 77-882: Excel 2010.

#	Objective
2.1	**Construct cell data**
	2.1.1 Use Paste Special
	2.1.1.1 Formats
3.1	**Apply and modify cell formats**
	3.1.1 Align cell content
3.2	**Merge or split cells**
	3.2.1 Use Merge & Center

Column width and row height

Explanation

You can apply various formats, such as borders and alignment, to customize the appearance of one or more cells in a row or column. You can also adjust the cell height and width. Doing so affects an entire row or column—you cannot change the height or width of an individual cell.

Excel automatically adjusts row height to accommodate the size of data in a row, while column widths need to be adjusted manually. There are several ways you can change column widths:

- **Drag the column border.** When you point to the border between two column headings, the pointer changes to a two-headed arrow. You can then drag the border to the left or right to decrease or increase the column width.

- **Double-click the column border.** This automatically sizes the column to fit the widest data it contains.

- **Set a specific numeric column size.** To do this, right-click a column label (or select multiple columns and then right-click) and choose Column Width. Then enter a width value and click OK.

The same options work for customizing row height.

AutoFit

You can use AutoFit to automatically adjust column widths and row heights. Select the column or row, display the Format menu in the Cells group, and choose the appropriate AutoFit option.

Setting the width of multiple columns

To set several contiguous columns to the same width, select the columns and then use one of the methods above to change the width. This method also works for setting row height.

B-1: Changing column width and row height

The files for this activity are in Student Data folder **Unit 5\Topic B**.

Here's how	Here's why
1 Open Outlander sales Save the workbook as **My Outlander sales**	
2 Select A1	The date in A4 does not fit within the default column width. Because the date was entered with a function, Excel displays a series of # symbols to indicate that data has been truncated.
3 Point to the border between column headings A and B	 The pointer changes to a two-headed arrow.
Press and hold the mouse button *If the date does not appear as students drag, have them drag a bit at a time until it does.* Drag slightly to the right until the date in A4 is visible	
4 Select column B	(Click column heading B.) You'll automatically size the column to fit the widest data it contains.
In the Cells group, click **Format**	To display the Format menu.
Choose **AutoFit Column Width**	To resize the column to fit the data. In this case, the column width decreases because Emp # is the widest data in the column and it's not as wide as the default column width.
5 Select columns C:F	(Drag over their column headings.) You'll resize these columns together.
6 Right-click the selection and choose **Column Width...**	To open the Column Width dialog box.
7 Type **7**	(In the Column Width box.) To specify that the selected columns should be seven characters wide.
Click **OK**	To change the width of the selected columns.

8 Select row 2	Click the row-2 label.
9 Right-click the selection and choose **Row Height...**	To open the Row Height dialog box.
Type **20** and click **OK**	To specify a row height of 20 points.
10 Save the workbook	

Applying color to rows and columns

Explanation

In addition to changing the row height or column width, you can add color to individual cells or entire rows or columns. You can change the text color and the cell background color (also called the *fill color*).

To apply a fill color to several rows or columns at once, first select the rows and/or columns. Then, on the Home tab, click the arrow on the Fill Color button in the Font group to open a color palette, and select the desired color.

Do it!

B-2: Applying color to a row

Here's how	Here's why
1 Select row 6	
2 In the Font group, click as shown	(The Fill Color arrow.) To open the color palette.
3 In the palette, select the pale green color	To apply the color to all cells in the row.
4 Apply the same color to row 16	(Select the row and click the Fill Color button.) The most recently used fill color is available to use again until you select another color.
Deselect the row	Click anywhere in the worksheet.
5 Save the workbook	

Students don't have to re-open the color palette to apply the same color that was previously used.

Alignment options

Explanation

Objective 3.1.1

Alignment in Excel refers to the location of data in a cell. For example, the data you type can be aligned to the left, right, or center of a cell. Data can also be aligned vertically at the top, bottom, or middle of a cell. By default, text is aligned to the left and bottom of the cell, while values are aligned to the right and bottom. To align the contents of a cell or a range of cells, select the cell or range and click an alignment button in the Alignment group, shown in Exhibit 5-3.

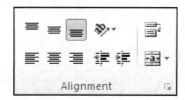

Exhibit 5-3: The alignment buttons in the Alignment group (on the Home tab)

The following table lists the buttons in the Alignment group.

Button	Button name
	Align Left
	Center
	Align Right
	Top Align
	Middle Align
	Bottom Align

Merge & Center

Objective 3.2.1

The Merge & Center button centers data over a range of cells (instead of within a single column). To use it, select the cell containing the data you want to merge and center, and select the rest of the cells over which you want to center the data. Then, in the Alignment group, click Merge & Center. For example, to center the text in B1 over columns A:F, select A1:F1 and click Merge & Center.

Do it!

B-3: Setting alignment

Here's how	Here's why
Objective 3.1.1	

The effect is subtle here; have students observe the cells as they click the button.

1 Select B6:H6

Click ☰ — (In the Alignment group.) To center the text within the cells.

2 Select G4 — This text is truncated. You'll change its alignment so that it is fully visible, without changing the column width.

Remind students that when there is no data in the adjacent cell, Excel displays overflowing text.

Click ☰ — (In the Alignment group.) To right-align the text in the cell. The part of the data that doesn't fit appears in the cell to the left, F4, because it does not contain any data.

3 Select A1:H1 — You'll center the worksheet title "Outlander Spices" over all of these cells.

Objective 3.2.1

Click ▦▾ — (The Merge & Center button is in the Alignment group.) To center the text in A1 over the entire range. There are no longer any cell borders within the selection because the cells in this range are merged into a single cell.

4 Center the text in A2 over A2:H2 — (Select A2:H2 and click the Merge & Center button.) To center the Bonus sales subheading over this entire range. Again, there are no cell gridlines in the merged range because they are now a single cell.

Again, the effect is subtle; have students observe the cells as they click the button.

With the merged cell in row 2 selected, click ☰ — (The Middle Align button is in the Alignment group.) To align the text in the middle of the cell.

5 Save the workbook

Cell borders

Explanation

Click the Borders button in the Font group to display a menu of border styles that you can apply to cells or ranges. (See Exhibit 5-4.) For more options, choose More Borders to open the Format Cells dialog box with the Border tab active.

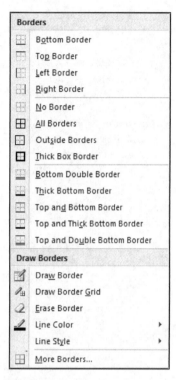

Exhibit 5-4: The Borders menu

Do it!

B-4: Applying borders to cell ranges

Here's how	Here's why
1 Select A6:H6	You'll put a heavy border below this text to separate it from the data below.
2 Click as shown	(In the Font group.) To display the Borders menu.
Choose **Thick Bottom Border**	
Deselect the range	(Click an empty cell.) To view the border.
3 Select A10:H10	You'll add a light border below this range to separate the employee data from the totals row.
4 Display the Borders menu	Click the arrow on the Borders button.
Choose **More Borders...**	To open the Format Cells dialog box with the Border tab active.

5 In the Style box, click as shown

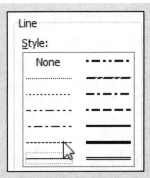

To select the dashed line.

6 Click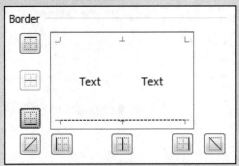

To make the dashed line a border for the bottom of the selected range.

Observe the Border preview

The Border preview shows a dashed line at the bottom.

Click **OK**

To apply the border and close the dialog box.

7 Deselect the range

To view the new border.

8 Save the workbook

The border-drawing pencil

Explanation

You can also draw borders around cells or ranges by using the border-drawing pencil.

1 Click the Borders button (in the Font group) to display the Borders menu.

2 Choose Draw Border, or choose a line color and line style. The pointer changes to a drawing pencil.

3 Drag where you want to apply a border.

Do it!

B-5: Using the border-drawing pencil

Here's how	Here's why
1 Display the Borders menu	You'll draw a border below a range of values.
Under Draw Borders, choose **Line Style**	To display the Line Style gallery.
2 Select a border style	The pointer changes to a pencil.
3 Drag the pencil under A4	To draw a border under this value.
Save the workbook	When you update the workbook, the pointer changes back to its default state.

Using Paste Special to copy and paste formatting

Explanation

Objective 2.1.1.1

You can copy and paste only formats if you don't want the actual contents of the copied cell or range. To do so, use either of the following methods:

- Copy the formatted cell or range, select the destination cell, display the Paste menu in the Clipboard group, and choose Formatting.
- Copy the formatted cell or range, select the destination cell, and right-click it. From the shortcut menu, choose Paste Special. In the Paste Special dialog box, under Paste, select "Formats." Click OK.

Pasting bordered data without the borders

You can copy and paste data in a bordered cell without pasting the border. To do so, use either of the following methods:

- Copy the bordered cell or range, select the destination cell, display the Paste menu in the Clipboard group, and choose No Borders.
- Copy the bordered cell or range, select the destination cell, and right-click it. From the shortcut menu, choose Paste Special. In the Paste Special dialog box, under Paste, select "All except borders." Click OK.

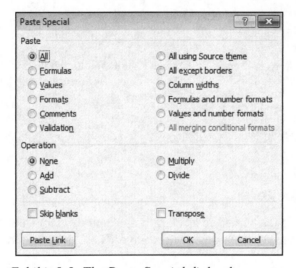

Exhibit 5-5: The Paste Special dialog box

Do it!

B-6:   Using the Paste Special command

Here's how	Here's why
1 Copy A4	Select it; then click the Copy button or press Ctrl+C.
2 Right-click A24	To display the shortcut menu.
3 Choose **Paste Special...**	To open the Paste Special dialog box, shown in Exhibit 5-5.
Under Paste, select **All except borders**	To remove the border when the value is pasted.
Click **OK**	To close the dialog box and paste the value. The border in A4 is not pasted into A24.
4 Copy A6:H11	To save time, you can copy the formatting from the northern region to the southern region.
Select A16	Because the destination range is the same size as the copied range, you only need to select the upper-right corner of the range.
Right-click A16, and under Paste Options, click [%]	(The Formatting button.) To paste the northern region's formatting onto the southern region.
5 Save the workbook	

Point out that this option retains the date formatting for the value.

Removing borders

Explanation

If you no longer want a border on a cell or range, you can remove it. Select the cell or range containing the border you want to remove. Then, from the Borders menu, choose No Border.

Do it!

B-7:   Removing a border

Here's how	Here's why
1 Select A4	You'll delete the border from this cell.
2 Display the Borders menu and choose **No Border**	To remove the borders from the selected cell.
3 Save and close the workbook	

Topic C: Number formatting

This topic covers the following Microsoft Office Specialist objectives for exam 77-882: Excel 2010.

#	Objective
3.1	**Apply or modify cell formats**
	3.1.2 Apply a number format

The Number group

Explanation

Numbers, including date and time data, can be displayed in many different formats. Actual cell values are not affected when you apply formatting.

Objective 3.1.2

Dollar signs ($), percent signs (%), and decimal places are examples of number formatting. By using number formats, you can make your worksheets easier to understand and call attention to specific data. The Number group, shown in Exhibit 5-6, provides several tools for formatting numbers.

Objective 3.1.2

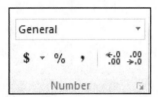

Exhibit 5-6: Number formatting options in the Number group

Button	Button name
$ ▾	Accounting Number Format
%	Percent Style
,	Comma Style
← .0 .00	Increase Decimal
.00 → .0	Decrease Decimal

Sometimes number formatting will make the data too wide to be displayed at the current column width. When this happens, Excel displays a series of number signs (#) instead of a truncated number. (This is done because the visible part of a truncated number might be mistaken for the complete number.) If number signs are displayed, either increase the column width or change the formatting of the number.

⊿	A	B	C	D	E	F	G	H
1			*Outlander Spices*					
2			*Bonus sales for the northern region*					
3								
4	10/27/2010 8:40						Comm_rate:	4%
5								
6	**Name**	**Emp #**	*Qtr1*	*Qtr2*	*Qtr3*	*Qtr4*	**Total**	**Comm**
7	Kendra James	16	6354	4846	3958	8284	$ 23,442	$ 938
8	Alan Monder	22	7546	6574	5767	6234	$ 26,121	$ 1,045
9	Audrey Kress	27	7635	4765	5256	7865	$ 25,521	$ 1,021
10	Julie George	29	9595	5859	4879	3432	$ 23,765	$ 951
11	**Totals**		$ 31,130	$ 22,044	$ 19,860	$ 25,815	$ 98,849	$ 3,954
12								

Exhibit 5-7: Totals formatted with commas and dollar signs

Do it!

C-1:   Using the Number group to format numbers

The files for this activity are in Student Data folder **Unit 5\Topic C**.

Objective 3.1.2

Here's how	Here's why
1 Open Regional	
Save the workbook as **My Regional**	
2 Select G7:H10	You'll format the numbers in these cells as currency.
Press and hold (CTRL), and select C11:H11	
3 Click as shown	(In the Number group.) To display the Currency gallery.
4 Select **$ English (U.S.)**	To format the numbers in G7:H11 as dollars, with two decimal places and a standard comma separating the thousands. Number signs (#) are displayed in row 11 because the values are too wide to fit in the cells.
5 Click [.00→.0] twice	(In the Number group.) To decrease the number of decimal places from two to zero. The numbers in C11:F11 are still too wide to be displayed.
6 Select columns C:H	(Drag over the column headings.) You'll resize the columns to fit the contents.
7 Point to the right border of the heading for column H, as shown	The pointer changes to a double-headed arrow.
Double-click the right border	The selected columns resize to fit the largest item in each column.
8 Select H4	The commission rate should be a percentage.
Click [%]	To format the cell data as a percentage.
9 Save the workbook	

Students might need to re-select the non-contiguous range.

The Format Cells dialog box

Explanation

Objective 3.1.2

The Number tab in the Format Cells dialog box offers a variety of number formats, including dates, times, fractions, and scientific notation, as shown in Exhibit 5-8. To open the Format Cells dialog box with the Number tab active, click the Dialog Box Launcher button in the Number group on the Ribbon.

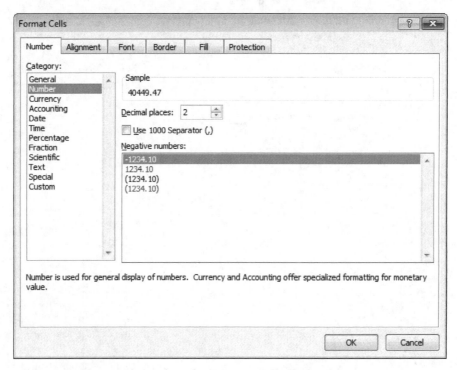

Exhibit 5-8: The Number tab in the Format Cells dialog box

Do it!   **C-2:   Exploring the Number tab**

Here's how	Here's why
1 Select A4	This cell uses a NOW function to return the current date and time. You'll change the format for the current date.
2 In the Number group, click ⬓	(The Dialog Box Launcher is in the bottom-right corner of the group.) The Format Cells dialog box opens with the Number tab active. Here, you can select a number format category. When a category is selected, related options are shown.
3 From the Category list, select **Number**	For numbers, you can specify how many decimal places to show and whether to display a comma as a thousands separator. You can also specify how you want negative numbers to appear.
4 From the Category list, select **Fraction**	To display the decimal value of a number as a fraction.
5 From the Category list, select **Date**	To display a list of date formats.
In the Type list, click as shown	
	(Scroll down.) To reformat the date and time field.
Click **OK**	To apply the formatting and close the dialog box. The date appears in the new format.
6 Save and close the workbook	

Objective 3.1.2

Point out that students are just exploring some options in this step and the next step.

Tell students to resize the column if the date isn't displayed properly.

Topic D: Conditional formatting

This topic covers the following Microsoft Office Specialist objectives for exam 77-882: Excel 2010.

#	Objective
8.3	**Apply conditional formatting**
	8.3.1 Apply conditional formatting to cells
	8.3.2 Use the Rule Manager to apply conditional formats
	8.3.4 Clear rules

Applying conditional formats

Explanation

Conditional formatting is formatting that's applied to data only if one or more specific conditions are met. You can use color or other formatting to highlight values that meet a condition that you set. For example, you can highlight in green all sales figures that exceed $75,000, or highlight in red all sales figures that do not meet a certain quota. You can apply conditional formatting based on a cell value or a formula.

To conditionally format data:

Objective 8.3.1

1 Select the cell or range containing the values to which you want to apply conditional formatting.

2 In the Styles group, click Conditional Formatting.

3 Do one of the following:

- Choose a condition and rule from the menu, shown in Exhibit 5-9.

- Choose New Rule. Then specify a condition and format in the New Formatting Rule dialog box, shown in Exhibit 5-10.

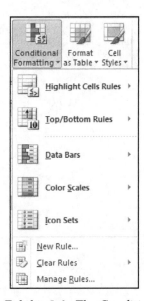

Exhibit 5-9: The Conditional Formatting menu

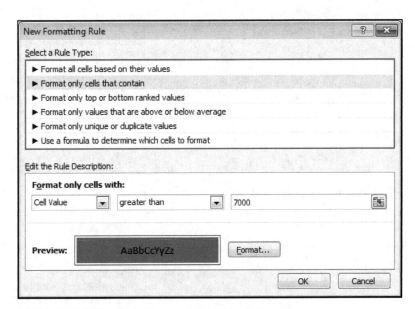

Exhibit 5-10: The New Formatting Rule dialog box

Do it!

D-1:   Creating a conditional format

The files for this activity are in Student Data folder **Unit 5\Topic D**.

Objectives 8.3.1, 8.3.2

Here's how	Here's why
1 Open Bonus data	
Save the workbook as **My Bonus data**	
2 Select C7:F10	You'll apply a conditional format that will highlight values if they're less than 4000.
3 In the Styles group, click **Conditional Formatting**	To display the Conditional Formatting menu.
Choose **Highlight Cells Rules**, **Less Than...**	To open the Less Than dialog box.
4 In the first box, type **4000**	**Format cells that are LESS THAN:** 4000
Press TAB	To move the insertion point to the fill list.
5 Observe the range	

6354	4846	3958	8284
7546	6574	5767	6234
7635	4765	5256	7865
9595	5859	4879	3432

Excel displays a preview of the formatting. Two cells that meet the condition are highlighted with a red fill and red text.

TIPS *Tell students they might have to move the dialog box to see the cells in the selected range.*

6 From the fill list, select **Custom Format...**

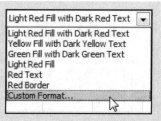

To open the Format Cells dialog box.

Click the **Fill** tab

You'll change the fill to yellow.

7 On the Background Color palette, click yellow, as shown

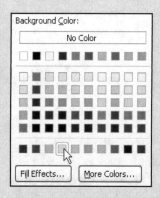

Click **OK**

To apply the yellow color and close the Format Cells dialog box.

8 Click **OK**

To apply the conditional format and close the Less Than dialog box.

Deselect the range

Cells E7 and F10 are yellow because the values they contain are less than 4000.

9 In D9, enter **3500**

To change Audrey Kress's Qtr2 sales figure. The cell now has a yellow background color.

10 Select C7:F10

You'll create a conditional format to highlight sales figures greater than 7000.

Click **Conditional Formatting** and choose **New Rule...**

To open the New Formatting Rule dialog box.

11 From the Select a Rule Type list, select **Format only cells that contain**

Under Edit the Rule Description, in the second box, select **greater than**

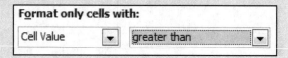

In the third box, enter **7000**

12 Under Preview, click **Format**	To open the Format Cells dialog box. Here you can choose a color to highlight cells with values matching your condition.
Click the **Fill** tab	
Select a blue color and click **OK**	To close the Format Cells dialog box.
13 Click **OK**	To apply the new rule and close the New Formatting Rule dialog box.
14 Deselect the range	Cells with a value greater than 7000 are highlighted with the selected color.
15 Select G7:G10	You'll highlight the top two earners.
Display the Conditional Formatting menu	
Choose **Top/Bottom Rules**, **Top 10 Items...**	To open the Top 10 Items dialog box.
In the first box, enter **2**	
16 Click **OK**	To close the dialog box and apply the default formatting to the top two totals in the column.
Deselect the range	The totals for Alan Monder and Audrey Kress are highlighted, making it easy to see who the top two earners are.
Save the workbook	

Modifying conditional formatting rules

Explanation

Objectives 8.3.2, 8.3.4

You can use the Rules Manager to edit or delete conditional formatting rules. To do so, click Conditional Formatting and choose Manage Rules. This opens the Rules Manager dialog box. Select the rule you want to modify or delete, and click OK.

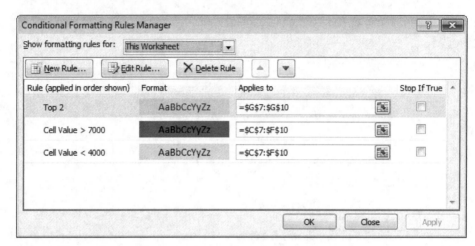

Exhibit 5-11: The Conditional Formatting Rules Manager

Do it!

D-2:   Editing and deleting a conditional format

Here's how	Here's why

Objective 8.3.2

1 Click **Conditional Formatting** and choose **Manage Rules...**

To open the Conditional Formatting Rules Manager dialog box.

2 From the "Show formatting rules for" list, select **This Worksheet**

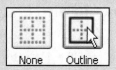

To display all rules in effect for the current worksheet, as shown in Exhibit 5-11.

3 From the list of rules, select **Top 2**

You'll edit the condition to display a border.

   Click **Edit Rule**

To open the Edit Formatting Rule dialog box.

4 Click **Format**

To open the Format Cells dialog box.

   Click the **Border** tab

   Click as shown

   Click **OK**

To close the Format Cells dialog box.

5 Click **OK**

To close the Edit Formatting Rule dialog box.

   Click **OK**

The cells containing the top two earners now have a border.

6 Open the Conditional Formatting Rules Manager

(Click Conditional Formatting and choose Manage Rules.) You'll delete a rule.

   Show the formatting rules for this worksheet

From the "Show formatting rules for" list, select This Worksheet.

7 From the list of rules, select **Top 2**

Objective 8.3.4

TIPS
Explain that the Clear Rules command can also be used to remove all rules from the selected cells or from the entire worksheet.

   Click **Delete Rule**

To delete the rule.

   Click **OK**

To close the Conditional Formatting Rules Manager and apply the change. Any cell formatting that was applied by this rule has been removed.

8 Save and close the workbook

Topic E: Additional formatting options

This topic covers the following Microsoft Office Specialist objectives for exam 77-882: Excel 2010.

#	Objective
2.2	**Apply AutoFill**
	2.2.3 Preserve cell formats
3.1	**Apply and modify cell formats**
	3.1.4 Use Format Painter
3.6	**Create and apply cell styles**
	3.6.1 Apply cell styles
8.2	**Sort data**
	8.2.1 Use Sort options
	8.2.1.1 Values

Copying and clearing formatting

Explanation

Objective 3.1.4

You can use the Format Painter to copy formats from one cell or range to other cells. This can save a lot of time, especially if you're working with multiple worksheets and you want to ensure that your data formatting is consistent.

1 Select the cell or range that has the formatting you want to copy.

2 In the Clipboard group on the Home tab, click Format Painter to copy the selection's formatting.

3 Select the cell or range to which you want to copy the formatting.

To clear formatting, select the cell or range you want to clear. In the Editing group, click the Clear button and choose Clear Formats.

Do it!

E-1: Copying formats

The files for this activity are in Student Data folder **Unit 5\Topic E**.

Here's how	Here's why
1 Open Outlander bonuses	
Save the workbook as **My Outlander bonuses**	
2 Select A2	You'll apply the formatting of this cell to A14.
Click [icon]	(The Format Painter button is in the Clipboard group.) To copy the formatting of the selected cell.
Click A14	To paste the copied formatting onto A14. The text is now formatted as a region subheading.
3 Copy the formatting for the entire northern region to the southern region data	Select A6:H11, click Format Painter, and select A16:H21.
4 Deselect the range	
5 Save the workbook	

Using AutoFill to copy formats

Explanation

In addition to using the Format Painter, you can use AutoFill to copy a format from one cell to another. To copy formatting by using AutoFill:

Objective 2.2.3

1 Select the cell containing the formats you want to copy.

2 Drag the fill handle in the bottom-right corner of the cell over the adjacent cells whose formatting you want to customize.

3 Click the Auto Fill Options button and select Fill Formatting Only.

Do it!

E-2:   Using AutoFill to copy formatting

Objective 2.2.3

Here's how	Here's why
1 Select B6	You'll copy only the formatting from this cell.
2 Drag the fill handle over C6:F6	The Emp # value is copied, along with the formatting.
3 Click as shown	
	To display the Auto Fill Options menu.
4 From the menu, choose **Fill Formatting Only**	To restore the original data but copy the formatting from B6.
5 Save and close the workbook	

Applying cell styles

Explanation

Cell styles are predefined combinations of text formats, number formats, borders, colors, and shading that you can apply in a single step. Cell styles can be applied to a single cell or a range of cells.

To apply a cell style:

Objective 3.6.1

1 Select a cell or range.
2 In the Styles group, click Cell Styles.
3 Move the pointer over the styles in the gallery—Live Preview shows how each style will affect the selected cell(s).
4 Click a style to select it.

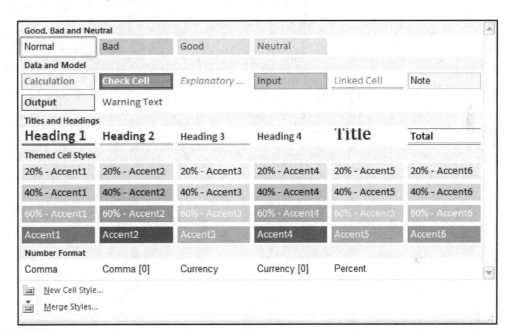

Exhibit 5-12: The Cell Styles gallery

Do it!

Objective 3.6.1

E-3: Applying cell styles

The files for this activity are in Student Data folder **Unit 5\Topic E**.

Here's how	Here's why
1 Open Northern	
Save the workbook as **My Northern**	
2 Select A1	If necessary.
3 In the Styles group, click **Cell Styles**	A gallery of built-in cell styles is displayed.
Move the pointer over the cell styles in the gallery	As you do, the cell you selected previews the cell styles.
4 Click as shown	Heading 4 Title
	To apply the Title style to the cell.

Applying table styles and sorting data

Explanation

Like cell styles, table styles are also predefined combinations of text formats, number formats, borders, colors, and shading that are applied with a single click. The difference is that table formats are intended for data that is arranged in a table.

To apply a table format:

1   Select a cell or range.
2   In the Styles group, click Format As Table.
3   Select a table style. The Format As Table dialog box opens.
4   Enter the range of the table (if necessary), and click OK. The Table Tools | Design tab appears and is active.
5   Use the Table Style Options and other groups on the Ribbon, as needed.
6   Click anywhere in the worksheet to close the Table Tools | Design tab.

Sorting table data

Objective 8.2.1.1

When data has been formatted as a table, you can easily sort it by using the arrows that appear next to the column headings. You can click an arrow to display a list of options for sorting, filtering, and hiding data.

E-4:   Applying table styles and sorting data

Here's how	Here's why
1 Select A6:H11	You'll apply a table style to the selection.
2 In the Styles group, click **Format As Table**	A gallery of built-in table styles is displayed.
Select the indicated table style	
	The Format As Table dialog box appears. Because you've already selected the range, the correct range appears in the dialog box.
Click **OK**	To apply the new style. The Ribbon changes to display the Table Tools | Design tab.
3 Observe the table	Each column has a menu button, which will display options for sorting, filtering, hiding, and showing data.
4 Click the arrow next to Total, as shown	
	To display the list of options.
Choose **Sort Smallest to Largest**	To sort the data in the table by the values in the Total column.
5 Click the arrow next to Name	You'll hide some of the table data.
Clear the checkbox for **Audrey Kress**	
	To hide the data in that row.
Click **OK**	The row with the data for Audrey Kress is now hidden. However, the totals and commission calculations are unaffected.
Show the hidden row	Click the arrow next to Name, check the box for Audrey Kress, and click OK.

Objective 8.2.1.1

After the table style is applied, the error indicator appears because Excel mistakenly thinks that the Emp # column data should be included in the formula. Students can ignore the error indicators.

6	Sort the table by employee number	(Click the arrow next to Emp # and choose Sort Smallest to Largest.) To return the table to its original sort order.
7	Save and close the workbook	

Changing formatting with Find and Replace

Explanation

You can use the Find and Replace dialog box to apply formatting to specific content. This feature is useful in a large worksheet where you cannot see every cell on screen at once, or when you want to change the formatting for multiple instances of a particular value or text string. You can also use this feature to change multiple instances of a particular format to a new format.

To use Find and Replace to change formatting:

1 In the Editing group (on the Home tab), click Find & Select and choose Replace. The Find and Replace dialog box opens.

2 Click Options to expand the dialog box. Then do either of the following:

- In the Find What box, type the data you want to search for.

- Next to the Find What box, click Format and then click Choose Format From Cell. Click the cell that has the formatting you want to change.

3 Click the second Format button to open the Replace Format dialog box. Select the formatting options you want to use, and click OK.

4 Click Replace All to update all instances of the data and/or formatting.

5 Click Close.

Do it!

E-5: Using Find and Replace to change formatting

The files for this activity are in Student Data folder **Unit 5\Topic E**.

Here's how	Here's why
1 Open Product managers	You'll use Find and Replace to format all instances of a product manager's name in a large worksheet.
Save the workbook as **My Product managers**	
2 In the Editing group, click **Find & Select**	To display the Find & Select menu.
Choose **Replace...**	To open the Find and Replace dialog box.
Click **Options**	To expand the dialog box.
3 In the Find What box, type **Melissa James**	You'll apply formatting to all instances of this name.
4 Click the second **Format** button, as shown	

To open the Replace Format dialog box.

Click the **Font** tab	
In the Font Style list, select **Bold Italic**	
Click **OK**	To select the format and close the dialog box.
5 In the Find and Replace dialog box, click **Replace All**	To change the formatting. A message box indicates the number of replacements made.
Click **OK**	
6 Click **Close**	To close the Find and Replace dialog box.
7 Scroll down the worksheet	To view the data. All cells that contain Melissa James's name are formatted in bold italics.
8 Save and close the workbook	

TIPS Tell students they can also press Ctrl+H.

Point out that you can also specify a format to search for and replace, rather than text or a value.

Unit summary: Formatting

Topic A In this topic, you learned how to format worksheets, including how to apply **text formatting**, such as boldface, italics, and font size. You learned how to select and format a **non-contiguous range**, and you learned that various text formatting options are available on the Font tab in the Format Cells dialog box.

Topic B In this topic, you learned how to **format rows and columns** and change column width and row height. You also learned how to align data in a cell, apply color to cells, and use the Merge & Center button to merge multiple cells into a single cell. Finally, you learned how to apply **borders** to cells.

Topic C In this topic, you learned how to **format numbers**. You learned how to apply currency and percentage formats and control the number of decimal places displayed for a number. You also learned how to use the Format Cells dialog box to apply additional number formats, including dates, times, fractions, and scientific notation.

Topic D In this topic, you learned how to apply **conditional formats** based on criteria you specify. You learned how to create, edit, and delete conditional formatting rules.

Topic E In this topic, you learned how to copy formatting by using the **Format Painter** and **AutoFill**. You also learned how to apply **table styles** and **sort** data. Finally, you learned how to use Find and Replace to change cell formatting.

Independent practice activity

In this activity, you'll use a variety of methods to format data in a workbook.

The files for this activity are in Student Data folder **Unit 5\Unit summary**.

1 Open Employee info and save it as **My Employee info**.

2 Format A1 as Times New Roman, bold, 18 pt, and center it over the range A1:E1.

3 Format A2 as Times New Roman, italic, 12 pt, and center it over the range A2:E2.

4 Format the range A4:E4 as bold, and apply a heavy border below it.

5 Add a thin border below row 12.

6 Center the contents of the range B4:E4 within their cells.

7 Resize column A so that you can see all the names in the column.

8 Format the range D5:D12 as currency with no decimal places.

9 Format the range E5:E12 as percentages with no decimal places.

10 Deselect the range and compare your work to Exhibit 5-13.

11 Apply a table style of your choice to the table data.

12 Save and close the workbook.

⊿	A	B	C	D	E
1	**Outlander Spices**				
2	*Employee information: Sales division*				
3					
4	**Name**	**Emp #**	**Region**	**Salary**	**Ret. plan**
5	Alan Monder	426587	Northern	$ 40,000	4%
6	Audrey Kress	422391	Northern	$ 38,000	2%
7	James Hanover	421424	Southern	$ 37,000	10%
8	Julie George	429192	Northern	$ 48,000	0%
9	Karen Anderson	426763	Southern	$ 44,000	6%
10	Kelly Palmatier	429669	Southern	$ 54,000	7%
11	Kendra James	426656	Northern	$ 37,000	12%
12	Michael Bobrow	424678	Southern	$ 52,000	0%

Exhibit 5-13: The workbook after Step 10

Review questions

1 What is a non-contiguous range?

A range of cells located in non-adjacent areas of the worksheet.

2 List three ways you can change the width of a column.

- *Drag the column border.*

- *Double-click the column border.*

- *Open the Column Width dialog box and enter a size.*

3 What is conditional formatting?

Conditional formatting makes it possible to apply a format only if a certain requirement is met, such as a negative number value or a positive value above a certain limit.

4 What are cell styles and table styles?

Predefined combinations of text formats, number formats, borders, colors, and shading that you can apply in a single step.

5 Describe two ways that you can use the Find and Replace dialog box to update formatting.

- *You can update the formatting of multiple instances of a particular value or text.*

- *You can change multiple instances of a particular format to a new format.*

Unit 6
Printing

Unit time: 45 minutes

Complete this unit, and you'll be able to:

A Preview how a worksheet will look when printed, use the spelling checker, and use Find and Replace to update data.

B Set page orientation, scaling, and margins, and create headers and footers.

C Print a worksheet and a selected range.

Topic A: Preparing to print

This topic covers the following Microsoft Office Specialist objectives for exam 77-882: Excel 2010.

#	Objective
4.3	**Manipulate workbook views**
	4.3.1 Use Normal workbook view
	4.3.2 Use Page Layout workbook view
	4.3.3 Use Page Break workbook view

Using the spelling checker

Explanation

Before printing a worksheet, you should preview it and check for spelling errors. Completing these tasks before you print can save time and paper.

The spelling checker finds and corrects spelling errors. You can check an entire worksheet or only part of a worksheet. When you check an entire worksheet, the spelling checker examines all elements, including cell contents, comments, graphics, and headers and footers. The search for errors begins at the selected cell, and Excel prompts you to continue from the beginning when it reaches the end of the worksheet.

The spelling checker will suggest possible corrections if the word it finds is close to an entry in the Excel dictionary. You can select a spelling option from the Suggestions box or enter your own correction.

You can also ignore a word that has been flagged by the spelling checker. For example, most names are not included in a dictionary. If the spelling checker flags a name or other word as a possible misspelling, you can ignore it, or you can add it to the dictionary so that the word is accepted the next time the spelling checker encounters it.

To check spelling in a worksheet or a range:

1. Click the Review tab.
2. In the Proofing group, click Spelling to open the Spelling dialog box. If there are any misspellings, the first one found is displayed.
3. Click Change to change the spelling to the option selected in the Suggestions list; click Add to Dictionary to add the word as originally written to the dictionary; or click Ignore All.
4. Continue through the worksheet or range by responding to the suggestions for each possible misspelling.
5. When the spelling check is complete, click OK to close the message box.

Do it!

A-1:   Checking spelling in a worksheet

The files for this activity are in Student Data folder **Unit 6\Topic A**.

Here's how	Here's why
1 Open Division sales	You'll check this worksheet for spelling errors.
Save the workbook as **My Division sales**	
2 Click the **Review** tab	To display the Reviewing tools.
3 Click **Spelling**	(In the Proofing group.) To open the Spelling dialog box. The text "Quaterly" appears in the Not in Dictionary box. The correct spelling of "Quarterly" appears in the Suggestions box.
4 Click **Change**	To correct the misspelled word and move on to the next item. "Burkhardt" appears in the Not in Dictionary box.
5 Click **Ignore All**	To prevent the Burkhardt name from being flagged as a misspelling in this worksheet. "Cardamon" appears next in the Not in Dictionary box.
6 Observe the Suggestions box	Two suggestions for correcting the spelling are displayed. "Cardamom" is selected.
Click **Change**	To correct the misspelling. The Spelling dialog box closes and a message box appears, stating that the spelling check is complete for the entire worksheet.
Click **OK**	To close the message box.

TIPS✔ *Students can also press F7 to open the Spelling dialog box.*

The Find and Replace dialog box

Explanation

When you need to replace specific values or text, it can be difficult to scroll through an entire worksheet to find each instance of that value or text, especially when the worksheet is large. To save time, you can use the Find and Replace dialog box to search for one or more occurrences of a specific value and replace it with a new value.

With the Find and Replace dialog box, you can search rows, columns, or an entire worksheet for formulas, values, or text, and replace each instance with the updated text or data. If you want to search only a range of cells, select the range and then proceed with the following steps.

To search for and replace values or text:

1   Click the Home tab.

2   In the Editing group, click Find & Select.

3   Choose Replace to open the Find and Replace dialog box.

4   In the Find what box, enter the value or text you want to find.

5   Click Find Next.

6   In the Replace with box, enter the new value or text.

7   Click Replace to replace the highlighted result of the search and to continue searching, or click Replace All to replace all instances of the value or text.

A-2: Finding and replacing text

Here's how	Here's why

1 Click the **Home** tab — You'll replace all instances of a name in the Product Manager list.

2 In the Editing group, click **Find & Select** — To display the Find & Select menu.

Choose **Replace...** — To open the Find and Replace dialog box.

In the Find what box, type **Melissa James** — (If necessary.) To search for this name, which needs to be replaced.

Click **Find Next** — G5 is selected because it contains the text you searched for.

3 In the Replace with box, type **Lee Jones** — To replace the text in G5 with the new text.

4 Click **Options** — To expand the dialog box.

Click the second **Format**, as shown — To open the Replace Format dialog box.

| No Format Set | Format... ▾ |
| No Format Set | Format... ▾ |

5 Click the **Font** tab

In the Font Style list, select **Italic** — To replace not only the text but also the typestyle.

Click **OK** — To close the dialog box.

6 In the Find and Replace dialog box, click **Replace** — Excel replaces the text in G5 with "Lee Jones," formats it in italics, and moves to the next instance.

7 Click **Replace All** — To replace all instances of "Melissa James" with "Lee Jones." A message box informs you that Excel has completed its search and made three replacements.

Click **OK** — To close the message box.

8 Click **Close** — To close the Find and Replace dialog box.

Save and close the workbook

Previewing a worksheet

Explanation

To preview a worksheet as it will look when printed, click the File tab and then click Print. Previewing a worksheet allows you to see how your page setup choices will affect a printout.

View options

Objectives 4.3.1–4.3.3

When you're viewing a worksheet normally, with the Home tab active, the status bar contains buttons that provide viewing options. The Normal View button is the default option. Click the Page Layout button to switch to Page Layout view, shown in Exhibit 6-1. You can drag the slider on the right side of the status bar to zoom in and out to see more pages or more detail. You can also click the Page Break Preview button to view and modify any page breaks in a worksheet.

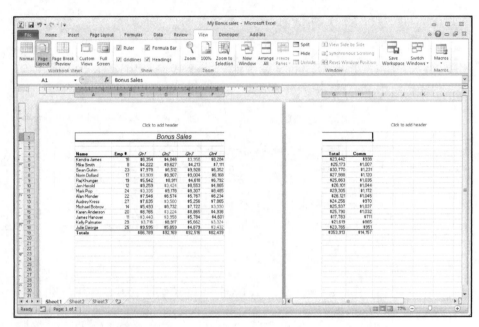

Exhibit 6-1: Page Layout view

Do it!

A-3:   Previewing a worksheet

The files for this activity are in Student Data folder **Unit 6\Topic A**.

Here's how	Here's why
1 Open Bonus sales	This workbook contains sales information for sales representatives.
2 Save the workbook as **My Bonus sales**	

⚠ It's not necessary for students' computers to be connected to a printer for this unit, but a printer must be set up on their computers.

3 Click the **File** tab	
Click **Print**	Several print options are displayed, and the preview of the page is displayed on the right.
Click as shown	
	(The Zoom to Page button is in the lower-right corner of the application window.) To zoom in on the page. You can use the scrollbars to see parts of the worksheet that do not fit inside the preview window.
Click the button again	To zoom out.
4 Click as shown	
	(The Show Margins button.) To display margin lines on the preview. You can adjust the margins by dragging the black boxes at the ends of the margin lines.
Click the button again	To turn off the Show Margins option.
5 Click as shown	
	To display the next page. The data is too wide to fit on a single page as currently configured, so the last column prints by itself on a separate page.
6 Click the **Home** tab	Next, you'll explore other page view options.
7 On the status bar, click [icon]	(The Page Layout View button.) To view the worksheet in Page Layout mode.
On the status bar, drag the Zoom slider bar slightly to the left	(If necessary.) To zoom out and view both pages in the worksheet.
8 Click [icon]	(The Normal View button.) To return to Normal view. This view was set to 100% zoom.
9 Save and close the workbook	

⚠ *Be sure students zoom out. Subsequent steps and activities depend on this.*

Objective 4.3.2

Help students find this button if necessary.

Objective 4.3.1

Topic B: Page Setup options

This topic covers the following Microsoft Office Specialist objectives for exam 77-882: Excel 2010.

#	Objective
1.2	**Print a worksheet or workbook**
	1.2.3 Construct headers and footers
	1.2.4 Apply printing options
	1.2.4.1 Scale
	1.2.4.3 Page setup
	1.2.4.4 Print area
	1.2.4.5 Gridlines
3.3	**Create row and column titles**
	3.3.1 Print row and column headings
	3.3.5 Configure titles to skip the first worksheet page
3.5	**Manipulate Page Setup options for worksheets**
	3.5.1 Configure page orientation
	3.5.2 Manage page scaling
	3.5.3 Configure page margins
	3.5.4 Change header and footer size

Page orientation and scaling

Explanation

The Print category on the File tab displays options that help you control several aspects of a worksheet's appearance and output.

On the File tab, click Print to display your print options, which include page orientation, collation, paper size, margins, and scaling. Portrait orientation is the default setting. You can change to Landscape orientation if you want to fit more data from left to right than from top to bottom. In other words, if your worksheet has multiple columns that are too wide to display in a standard (vertical) page layout, you can choose Landscape orientation to print the worksheet sideways on the page. You can also change page orientation from the Page Layout tab.

Objectives 1.2.4.1, 3.5.1

If you prefer not to use Landscape orientation, you can change scaling settings to fit your data. At the bottom of the print options, click No Scaling (the default setting) and choose either Fit All Columns on One Page or Fit Sheet on One Page, depending on which is better suited for your worksheet. As you change print setup options, the preview window shows you how your worksheet will look when printed.

You can also control scaling on the Page Layout tab. In the Scale to Fit group, click the arrow on the Width box and choose 1 page. This forces all columns to fit onto one page. You can also enter a specific value in the Scale box to apply custom scaling.

Do it!

B-1: Setting page orientation and scaling

The files for this activity are in Student Data folder **Unit 6\Topic B**.

Objectives 1.2.4.1, 3.5.1, 3.5.2

Here's how	Here's why
1 Open Total sales	
Save the workbook as **My Total sales**	
2 Click the **File** tab	
Click **Print**	To display the print options.
Objective 3.5.1 3 Under Settings, click **Landscape Orientation**	◄ 1 of 4 ► The bottom of the preview displays the current page and the total number of pages in the printout. You can click the Next Page arrow to view page 2.
Choose **Portrait Orientation**	To make the worksheet print on two pages.
Objectives 1.2.4.1, 3.5.2 4 At the bottom of the print options, click **No Scaling**	(You might need to scroll down.) To display a menu of scaling options.
Choose **Fit Sheet on One Page**	The preview shows the data now fitting on one page. When you have more data than will fit on a page, you can use this option to quickly solve the problem, rather than having to directly change column widths.
5 Click **Save**	To save the worksheet and activate the Home tab.
6 Click the **Page Layout** tab	You can also control page orientation and scaling here, but there is no Live Preview while you make adjustments.
The worksheet is scaled to 62%. In the Scale to Fit group, observe the current settings	Width: 1 page Height: 1 page Scale: 62% Scale to Fit The previous command scaled the worksheet down to fit all columns on one printed page.

Margins

Explanation

*Objectives 1.2.4.3,
3.5.3*

A *margin* is the space between the edge of a page (worksheet) and its content. There are four of these: the top, bottom, left, and right margins. In the Page Setup group (on the Page Layout tab), you can click Margins to select from a list of typical margin settings, or you can click Custom Margins to open the Page Setup dialog box, shown in Exhibit 6-2. There, you can enter custom margin values for all four sides. You can also use the "Center on page" options to center the data horizontally or vertically.

Tell students that depending on the printer being used, different options might be available.

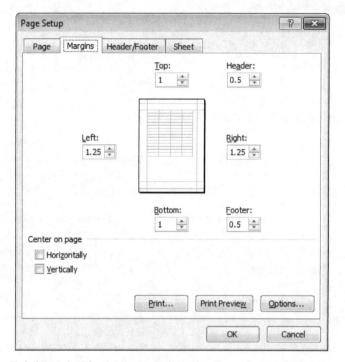

Exhibit 6-2: The Margins tab in the Page Setup dialog box

Do it!

Objectives 1.2.4.3, 3.5.3

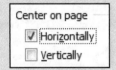

The Page Layout tab is active.

B-2:   Adjusting margins

Here's how	Here's why
1 In the Page Setup group, click **Margins**	To display the Margins gallery. Several standard margin setups are listed.
Choose **Narrow**	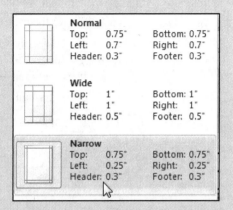
2 In the Page Setup group, click ▣	(The Dialog Box Launcher is in the bottom-right corner of the group.) To open the Page Setup dialog box.
Click the **Margins** tab	You can set the left, right, top, bottom, header, and footer margins to specific values (measured in inches). You can also center the data on the page.
3 Under "Center on page," check **Vertically**	To specify that you want to center the data vertically on the page. The preview shows how the data will look.
Clear **Vertically**	To move the data back to the top of the page.
4 Check **Horizontally**	Center on page ☑ Horizontally ☐ Vertically
	To center the data horizontally on the page.
Click **OK**	To apply the margin settings and return to the worksheet.
5 Observe the Scale box	(In the Scale to Fit group.) With narrow margins, the worksheet will be printed at a slightly higher zoom setting. However, it's not significant enough, so we'll remove the scaling.
6 Click the **File** tab and click **Print**	To display print options and a print preview.
Under Settings, remove the scaling setting	Click Fit Sheet on One Page and choose No Scaling.
7 Save the workbook	

Headers and footers

Explanation

A header and footer on each page can provide important information about a worksheet, such as the current date, page number, author, workbook or worksheet name, company logo, or combinations of these and other options.

Objective 1.2.3

To add a header or footer:

1   Click the Insert tab.

2   In the Text group, click Header & Footer. Page Layout view is activated, with the Header & Footer Tools | Design tab displayed. An empty header box appears in the top center of the first page.

3   Add text and any other elements you want to include.

You can add items from the Header & Footer Elements group on the Header & Footer Tools | Design tab. These elements are shown in Exhibit 6-3.

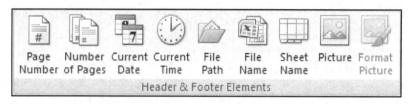

Exhibit 6-3: The Header & Footer Elements group

You can place text or other elements in the left, center, or right sections of a header or footer, as shown in the example in Exhibit 6-4. You can move between these sections by pressing Tab to move to the right, or Shift+Tab to move to the left.

Objective 1.2.3

Sales division	Outlander Spices|	Page 1 of 1

Bonus Sales

Exhibit 6-4: Header elements in the left, center, and right sections

Do it!

B-3:   Creating headers and footers

Objective 1.2.3

Here's how	Here's why
1 Click the **Insert** tab	
Point out that the text might be difficult to read in the current view. 2 In the Text group, click **Header & Footer**	Page Layout view is activated and the Header & Footer Tools	Design tab is displayed. The insertion point automatically moves to a header box in the center of the first page.
3 Type **Outlander Spices**	To add header text that is centered on the page.
4 Press (SHIFT) + (TAB)	To move to the left header box.
Type **Sales division**	Header Sales division
	To add header text that is aligned to the left side of the page.

5 Press TAB twice	To move to the right header box. You'll add a header that combines text and predefined elements.
6 Type **Page**	
Point out that students won't see the space being added in the header.	
Press SPACEBAR	To add a space between the word "Page" and the element that will follow it.
Click **Page Number**	Page &[Page]
	(In the Header & Footer Elements group.) To insert the "&[Page]" element, which will print the current page number.
7 Press SPACEBAR	
Type **of** and press SPACEBAR	
Point out that these elements appear as variables while you're editing the footer elements.	
8 Click **Number of Pages**	Page &[Page] of &[Pages]
	(In the Header & Footer Elements group.) To insert the "&[Pages]" element, which will print the total number of pages in the worksheet.
9 In the Navigation group, click **Go to Footer**	The insertion point automatically moves to the lower-right section of the footer.
Click **Current Date**	(In the Headers & Footer Elements group.) The "&[Date]" element enters a date function that will show the current date when the file is opened.
Click **Go to Header**	To display the header boxes again.
TIPS ✓ Students can use the Zoom to Page button, in the lower-right corner of the window, to see the header and footer better.	
10 Click the **File** tab and click **Print**	To preview the worksheet and its header and footer elements.
Click **Next Page**	◀ 1 of 2 ▶
	To view page 2. In a multi-page worksheet, the page-number elements change automatically to indicate the current page number and the total number of pages in the worksheet.
11 Save the workbook	

Formatting headers and footers

Explanation

Objective 3.5.4

To format text and other elements in the header and footer, you can use the Font group and other formatting tools on the Home tab. To increase the font size of the header text, do the following:

1 Select the header text.

2 On the Home tab, in the Font group, click the Grow Font button or select a new font size from the Font Size list.

You can also change the header and footer margins. To do so, open the Page Setup dialog box and click the Margins tab. Use the spinner controls to increase or decrease the margin settings.

Printing different headers and footers

Objectives 3.3.4, 3.3.5

You can specify different headers and footers for the first page, odd-numbered pages, and even-numbered pages.

Suppressing the first-page header and footer

On the Header & Footer Tools | Design tab, in the Options group, check Different First Page. You can leave the first-page header and footer sections blank so that no headers or footers are printed on the first worksheet page.

Using different odd and even headers and footers

To specify different header and footer text or alignment for odd and even pages, check the Different Odd & Even Pages checkbox in the Options group, on the Header & Footer Tools | Design tab. Then enter the desired text in the desired header and footer sections.

Do it!   **B-4:   Formatting headers and footers**

Here's how	Here's why
1 Click the **Home** tab	If necessary.
2 Select the **Outlander Spices** header	Outlander Spices
From the Font Size list, select **14**	To increase the size of the header text.
3 Increase the font size of the other two headers to **14**	Select the header text and then select 14 from the Font Size list.
4 Preview the worksheet	(Click the File tab and click Print.) On the first page, the header competes with the titles near the top of the worksheet. We'll suppress the headers on the first page only.
Save the worksheet	To save your header text changes and return to the Home page.
5 Verify that the header is still selected	
Click the **Design** tab	Under Header & Footer Tools.
Objective 3.3.5 — 6 In the Options group, check **Different First Page**	Header & Footer Tools Add-Ins Design ☑ Different First Page ☑ Scale with Do ☐ Different Odd & Even Pages ☑ Align with Pa
	We'll leave the first-page header boxes empty.
7 Click **Go to Footer**	To activate the right footer section. It would be helpful to have the current date in the first-page footer.
In the Header & Footer Elements group, click **Current Date**	To insert the date element.
8 Preview the worksheet	The first page looks better.
View the second page	(Click Next Page.) The header text appears on the second page. Only the footer is on every page.
Save the worksheet	

Sheet options

Explanation

Objective 1.2.4.5

The Sheet tab of the Page Setup dialog box (shown in Exhibit 6-5) is useful for multi-page worksheets. You can use the Print titles section to define row or columns that should be repeated on every page of the printout. You can specify the order in which Excel prints sections of the worksheet, and select other print options for the current worksheet.

Exhibit 6-5: The Sheet tab in the Page Setup dialog box

Gridlines and column and row headings

Objectives 1.2.4.5, 3.3.1

There may be times when you'll want to see just the data on a worksheet, and not the gridlines or column and row headings. To hide these elements, click the Page Layout tab on the Ribbon. In the Sheet Options group, under both Gridlines and Headings, clear the checkbox next to View.

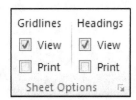

Exhibit 6-6: The Sheet Options group on the Page Layout tab

Do it!

B-5:   Printing gridlines and headings

Objectives 1.2.4.5, 3.3.1

Here's how	Here's why
1 Click the **Page Layout** tab	
In the Sheet Options group, under Gridlines, clear **View**	To hide the gridlines on the worksheet.
2 Display the gridlines	In the Sheet Options group, under Gridlines, check View.
3 Under Gridlines, check **Print**	To print the gridlines.
4 Under Headings, check **Print**	To print the row and column headings.
5 In the Sheet Options group, click ▣	(The Dialog Box Launcher is in the bottom-right corner of the group.) To open the Page Setup dialog box.
Click the **Sheet** tab	If necessary.
Observe the Print section	As shown in Exhibit 6-5, the print quality setting and other options appear here.
6 Observe the Page order section	You can specify the order in which worksheet areas are divided into printable pages.
7 Preview the worksheet	Click Print Preview in the dialog box.
Save and close the workbook	

Topic C: Printing worksheets

This topic covers the following Microsoft Office Specialist objectives for exam 77-882: Excel 2010.

#	Objective
1.2	**Print a worksheet or workbook**
	1.2.1 Print only selected worksheets
	1.2.2 Print an entire workbook
	1.2.4 Apply printing options
	1.2.4.4 Print area

Selecting printing options

Explanation

Objectives 1.2.1, 1.2.2

When you're satisfied with your worksheet and you have prepared it for printing, it's easy to print it.

When you're ready to print, click the File tab and then click Print, or simply press Ctrl+P. On the Print page, you can select the printer you want to use (if more than one printer is available), and apply other settings such as page orientation, margins, and scaling. You can also choose to print the active sheet, the entire workbook, or the current selection.

Printing a selection

To print only a range of cells:

1. Select the range you want to print.
2. Click the File tab and then click Print.
3. Under Settings, click Print Active Sheets (the default selection) and choose Print Selection.
4. Click Print.

Setting a print area

Objective 1.2.4.4

If you frequently print a selected range of cells, you can define that selection as a print area. Then, when you print the worksheet, only the print area is printed. You can add cells to the print area, or clear the print area to print the entire worksheet.

To set a print area:

1. Select the range to be printed.
2. On the Page Layout tab, in the Page Setup group, click Print Area and choose Set Print Area.
3. Click the File tab and click Print to verify that only the print area will be printed.

C-1: Printing a selected range

The files for this activity are in Student Data folder **Unit 6\Topic C**.

Objectives 1.2.1, 1.2.2

Here's how	Here's why
1 Open Regions	
Save the worksheet as **My Regions**	
2 Select A1:F41	You'll print only this selected range.
3 Press CTRL + P	To display printing options. The selection is displayed in the preview area.
Under Settings, verify that **Print Active Sheets** is active	Even though a range is selected, Excel assumes that you want to print the active worksheet.
Observe the bottom of the Print Preview screen	This worksheet requires four pages to print.
4 Click **Print Active Sheets**	To display the other options. You can print the active sheets, the entire workbook, or just the current selection.
Choose **Print Entire Workbook**	The number of pages remains at 4 because there is only one worksheet in this workbook.
5 Click the **Page Layout** tab	Verify that A1:F41 is still selected.
6 In the Page Setup group, click **Print Area**	
Choose **Set Print Area**	To define A1:F41 as the print area.
7 Click the **File** tab and click **Print**	
Observe the print settings	Even though Print Entire Workbook is selected, only the print area will be printed. If there were additional worksheets in this workbook, then they would be printed as well.
8 Save and close the workbook without printing	If you were going to print the worksheet, you would click Print instead.

Objective 1.2.4.4

Point out that if students wanted to print the worksheet, they would click Print.

Unit summary: Printing

Topic A   In this topic, you learned how to check for misspelled words by using the **spelling checker**. You also learned how to use **Find and Replace** to update text or values. You learned how to **preview** a worksheet and show margins in the Preview window.

Topic B   In this topic, you learned how to use controls on the **Page Layout** tab and in the **Page Setup** dialog box. You learned how to set page orientation, scaling, and margins. Then you learned how to create and format **headers and footers**, and print gridlines and headings.

Topic C   In this topic, you learned how to **print** a worksheet and a selected range. You learned that you can press Ctrl+P to display printing options, and then select the settings you want.

Independent practice activity

In this activity, you'll preview a worksheet, change the page orientation, scale the worksheet to fit on one page, create custom headers and footers, and print a worksheet.

The files for this activity are in Student Data folder **Unit 6\Unit summary**.

1 Open Sales report and save it as **My Sales report**.

2 Display the Print screen.

3 Adjust the scaling so that the entire sheet fits on one page.

4 Select Landscape Orientation.

5 Create a custom header. In the center section, enter **Outlander Spices**. In the left section, insert a Current Date element.

6 Click Go to Footer. In the right section, insert a File Name element.

7 Click the File tab and then click Print.

8 Zoom in and observe the header and footer.

9 Zoom out and apply a narrow margin.

10 Compare your worksheet to Exhibit 6-7.

11 Save and close the workbook.

Name	Emp#	Jan	Feb	Mar	Apr	May	Jun	Jul	Aug	Sep	Oct	Nov	Dec	Total	Comm
Kendra James	16	6354	7975	3227	8296	7995	9529	7576	7766	7083	4846	3956	8284	$ 82,868	$ 3,315
Mike Smith	8	4222	3635	3806	9902	9838	8057	8699	4807	7405	9627	4213	7111	$ 81,022	$ 3,241
Sean Guhin	23	7978	3380	9945	4368	6040	3521	6667	5597	7350	6512	9928	6352	$ 77,238	$ 3,090
Norin Dollard	17	3909	3838	9565	5563	7164	3237	3850	5815	6841	8907	9004	6166	$ 73,561	$ 2,946
Raj Khunger	19	5542	9765	8888	6470	7390	6975	8941	8179	4357	8911	4618	6792	$ 86,838	$ 3,474
Jen Herold	12	9259	5222	7283	3530	9393	4243	3932	6854	8367	3424	8553	4865	$ 76,925	$ 3,077
Mark Pop	24	3335	4443	4590	3824	5662	8208	8285	6069	4704	9178	8307	8485	$ 75,090	$ 3,004
Alan Monder	22	7546	5145	3447	5228	8272	9197	8960	6747	3439	6574	5767	6234	$ 76,556	$ 3,062
Audrey Kress	27	7835	7257	9750	4702	7440	7411	6757	4728	9868	3500	5256	7865	$ 82,169	$ 3,287
Michael Bobrow	14	5493	4813	6079	8254	8652	6214	9393	4035	5149	8732	7722	3990	$ 77,526	$ 3,101
Karen Anderson	20	8765	8248	4309	3360	7233	5841	9036	7442	3683	3224	8865	4936	$ 74,942	$ 2,998
James Hanover	11	3440	5087	3737	9872	3955	7737	5589	3875	9730	3956	5784	4601	$ 67,365	$ 2,695
Kelly Palmater	29	3716	8753	5872	7883	7756	5137	5065	9696	4421	8917	5662	3324	$ 76,205	$ 3,048
Julie George	25	9695	9770	9654	8290	8944	9470	5490	7977	4428	5859	4879	3432	$ 87,686	$ 3,507
Totals		86789	87131	89452	89542	105734	94777	98341	91388	86813	92169	92516	82439	$1,096,091	$ 43,844

10/27/2010 — Outlander Spices — Annual Sales Report — My Sales report

Exhibit 6-7: The completed worksheet

Review questions

1 True or false? When you select a range of cells and then press Ctrl+P to display print options, you can print only the selected range.

False. Excel will assume that you want to print only the selected range, but you can still print the full worksheet or the entire workbook.

2 True or false? Using the Find and Replace dialog box, you can replace text, values, and even formulas.

True. You can also replace formatting.

3 Describe two ways you can make a worksheet with several columns print on one page.

In the printing options, you can select Landscape Orientation. If that's not enough to accommodate all columns, you can scale the worksheet to fit all columns on one page.

4 What is a margin?

Margins are the spaces between the edges of a page (worksheet) and its content.

Unit 7

Charts

Unit time: 40 minutes

Complete this unit, and you'll know how to:

A Create charts based on worksheet data, and move charts within a workbook.

B Customize charts and format chart elements.

Topic A: Chart basics

This topic covers the following Microsoft Office Specialist objective for exam 77-882: Excel 2010.

#	Objective
6.1	Create charts based on worksheet data

Creating and moving a chart

Explanation

Charts are graphic representations of data. A chart can often communicate information more effectively than a table full of numbers can. For example, it takes time to notice a trend in a table of data, but a sloping graph in a chart communicates the trend instantly.

You can create charts based on the data in a worksheet. A chart can be an object embedded in a worksheet or placed on a separate chart sheet in a workbook.

To create a chart:

Objective 6.1

1   Select the data that you want to include in the chart. This data should include all values you want to display in the chart, plus any text that identifies those values.

2   On the Ribbon, click the Insert tab.

3   In the Charts group, click the desired chart type; then choose a sub-type from the gallery to insert the chart in the worksheet.

4   While the chart is selected, Excel displays three Chart Tools contextual tabs, labeled Design, Layout, and Format. Use the options on these tabs to format and customize the chart as needed.

5   If necessary, move the chart to the desired location on the worksheet. To move a chart, point to an empty area in it or to a chart border, and drag it.

Chart data

There is a link between the data from which you create a chart and the chart itself. Therefore, if you update any of the source data, the change is reflected immediately in any charts based on that data.

Do it!

A-1:   Creating a chart

The files for this activity are in Student Data folder **Unit 7\Topic A**.

Objective 6.1

Here's how	Here's why
1 Open 2010 sales	This workbook contains some simple data from which you'll create some charts.
Save the workbook as **My 2010 sales**	
2 Select A4:E8	This is the range for which you'll create a chart.
3 Click the **Insert** tab	
In the Charts group, click **Column**	To open the Column gallery.

4	Observe the column types	There are 2-D and 3-D columns, and Cylinder, Cone, and Pyramid charts.
	In the Charts group, click **Line**	To open the Line gallery. Thumbnail images of the available line charts are displayed.
	Point to each thumbnail	(In the Charts gallery.) To read the ScreenTip that appears for each line chart. Reviewing these can help you choose the best chart type for your particular data.
5	Click **Column**	You'll create a column chart.
	Click as shown	To insert a 3-D Clustered Column chart.
6	Observe the Ribbon	The Ribbon displays three Chart Tools tabs: Design, Layout, and Format.
7	Click the **Layout** tab	(Under Chart Tools.) This tab provides selections for customizing your chart.
8	In the Labels group, click **Chart Title**	To display the gallery of chart titles.
	Choose **Above Chart**	To place a centered title above the chart.
9	Triple-click **Chart Title**	To select the default text.
	Type **2010**	
10	Point to an empty area on the chart	The pointer changes to a four-headed arrow, indicating that you can move the chart in any direction.
	Drag the chart to the right	So that it doesn't overlap any data.
11	Edit B8 to read **2000**	
	Observe the chart	It has been updated to reflect the changed data. The column that was the tallest is now the shortest.
	Click	To undo the data edit and update the chart.
	Save the workbook	

Moving charts within workbooks

Explanation

In addition to moving a chart on a worksheet, you can move a chart to a separate sheet, known as a chart sheet. A chart sheet shows only the chart, not the data from which it was drawn.

To move a chart to a separate chart sheet:

1   Click the chart to select it and to display the Chart Tools tabs.
2   Click the Design tab.
3   In the Location group, click Move Chart to open the Move Chart dialog box.
4   Select New sheet, and enter a name for the chart sheet. (Excel provides a default name that you can edit.)
5   Click OK.

To move a chart from a chart sheet to a worksheet, open the Move Chart dialog box, select Object in, and select the worksheet in which you want to place the chart.

Do it! **A-2: Moving a chart within a workbook**

Here's how	Here's why
1 Select the chart	To display the Chart Tools tabs.
Click the **Design** tab	You'll move the chart to a new sheet.
2 In the Location group, click **Move Chart**	To open the Move Chart dialog box.
Select **New sheet**	To create a chart sheet.
Edit the name to read **Bonus Chart**	⊙ New <u>s</u>heet: Bonus Chart To name the new chart sheet.
Click **OK**	The new chart sheet is displayed.
3 If necessary, zoom out so that the chart fits in the window	Click the Zoom percentage on the status bar, choose Fit selection in the Zoom dialog box, and click OK.
4 Observe the worksheet tabs in the status bar	A new sheet tab named Bonus Chart appears before the default sheets.
5 Select the chart	You'll move the chart back into the worksheet.
Click **Move Chart**	In the Location group, on the Design tab.
6 Select **Object in**	
Verify that **Sheet1** appears in the list, and click **OK**	To close the dialog box and place the chart as an object in Sheet1. The Bonus Chart sheet is removed.
7 Drag the chart to the right of the heading and data	
8 Save the workbook	

Depending on the size of their screens, students might not need to do this step.

Students will now move the chart back to the original worksheet.

Chart elements

Explanation   The following table describes common chart elements.

Chart element	Description
Value axis	Provides the scale for all data points in the chart, based on the values in the selected range.
Category axis	Identifies the categories in the chart, as defined in the first row of data in the selected range.
Data point	Is a value from one cell in the selected range.
Data series	Comprises the values from all cells in a category.
Legend	Identifies the data series in the chart.

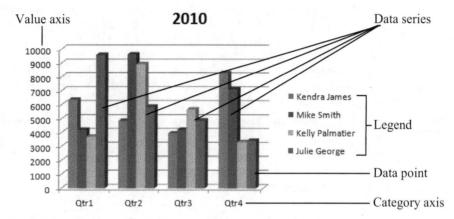

Exhibit 7-1: Chart elements

Do it!

A-3: Examining chart elements

Here's how	Here's why
1 Point to the first column bar in Qtr1	A ScreenTip appears. This data point is from the data series for Kendra James. The data point is for Qtr1, and the value is 6,354. In this chart, each column represents a data point.
2 Point to the first column bar for each quarter	These four columns make up a series—Kendra James's sales in all four quarters. Each series in this chart represents the sales figures for an individual sales rep.
3 Observe the legend	■ Kendra James ■ Mike Smith ▨ Kelly Palmatier ■ Julie George The data for the legend is pulled from the first column of the data selected for the series.
4 Observe the category axis	The categories in this chart are pulled from the first row of data selected for the series.
5 Observe the value axis	The scale for the value axis is generated automatically based on the minimum and maximum data points in the selected range.

Pie charts

Explanation

Pie charts are a popular data presentation format. Pie charts reveal the relative size of data points within a single data series. The pie is the sum of all data points in the series; each data point presents a percentage of the whole pie.

However, pie charts are typically not an effective chart type to use when one or more values in your data series are zero or negative values—these can't be represented visually in a pie chart. Also, too many categories can result in overly small pie slices that don't communicate effectively.

Do it!

Objective 6.1

Help students find the Sheet2 tab, if necessary.

A-4: Creating and editing a pie chart

Here's how	Here's why
1 Click **Sheet2**	To display the second worksheet in this workbook. You'll create a pie chart showing the percentage of the budget for each department.
2 Select A4:A9	This range will supply the text for the legend in the chart.
Press and hold CTRL , and select C4:C9	

Department	% Yearly budget
Marketing	23%
Sales	25%
Human Resources	12%
Customer Support	10%
Other	30%

To add the %Yearly budget column to the selection. This column will provide the data for the chart.

3 Click the **Insert** tab	
In the Charts group, click **Pie**	

Tell students that pie charts are especially useful for showing percentages of a total.

Click as shown

To create a 3-D pie chart. The Chart Tools tabs are displayed.

4 Click the **Format** tab

In the Size group, click the Dialog Box Launcher, as shown

To open the Size and Properties dialog box. The Size category is active.

5	Under Scale, change the Width value to **80%**		To decrease the chart's width.
	Click **Close**		To apply the new chart size.
6	Drag the chart to the area below the data		(Point to an empty area on the chart and drag.) So that you can see the data table and the chart.
7	Edit C5 to read **50%**		
	Edit C9 to read **3%**		The total must be 100%.
	Observe the change in the chart		The pie chart changes because it's linked to the worksheet data.
8	Click a blank area of the chart		To select it.
	Click the **Design** tab		Under Chart Tools.
	In the Chart Layouts group, click as shown		
			To scroll down to view other chart layouts.
9	Select the indicated chart layout	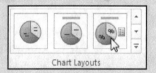	
	Observe the chart	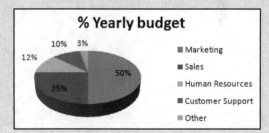	

In this chart layout, the percentage values are displayed on or near their corresponding pie wedges.

10 Save and close the workbook

Topic B: Formatting charts

Explanation

You can modify charts in a variety of ways, including changing the chart type, applying various predefined styles and layouts, and customizing labels.

Chart types

To change a chart's type, select the chart. Click the Chart Tools | Design tab and then click Change Chart Type (in the Type group). This opens the Change Chart Type dialog box, which contains a gallery of chart types. Select a chart type and click OK.

Chart styles and layouts

In addition to chart types, there are many predefined styles and layouts that you can apply to your charts. To do so, select the chart and click the Chart Tools | Design tab. Then select an option from the Chart Styles group or the Chart Layouts group. (Use the scrollbar in each group to see the options not shown by default on the Ribbon.)

Do it!

B-1:   Applying chart types and chart styles

The files for this activity are in Student Data folder **Unit 7\Topic B**.

Here's how	Here's why
1 Open 2010 bonuses	
Save the workbook as **My 2010 bonuses**	
2 Click the chart	To select it. The Chart Tools tabs appear on the Ribbon.
3 Click the **Design** tab	(Under Chart Tools.) You'll apply a different chart type.
In the Type group, click **Change Chart Type**	To open the Change Chart Type dialog box.
4 From the Chart Type list, select **Bar**	To display the bar chart options. Bar charts are like horizontal column charts.
Select the indicated type	To change the chart to a Clustered Horizontal Cylinder.

5 Click **OK**

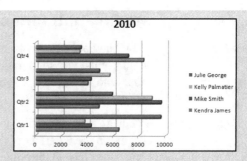

To close the dialog box and apply the change.

6 Click the chart style shown

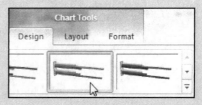

(In the Chart Styles group.) To change the bar styles to different shades of blue.

7 Click **Change Chart Type**

In the Type group.

Click **Column**

To display the column options.

8 Point to the options in the first row

To read the ScreenTips, which provide brief descriptions of the chart types.

Select the 3-D Clustered Column, as shown

Click **OK**

Adding and formatting chart elements

Explanation

You can apply formatting to various chart elements, including labels, legends, titles, and data points. For some elements, you have several formatting options, such as position, font, and font size. To format a chart element, right-click it and choose a formatting option.

You can also select chart elements from the drop-down list in the Current Selection group on the Chart Tools | Format tab. You can then format the selection by using options in the Shape Styles, WordArt Styles, Arrange, and Size groups on the Ribbon.

Axis titles

You can add axis titles to provide important information about your data. To add an axis title to a chart:

1 Select the chart.
2 Click the Layout tab.
3 In the Labels group, click Axis Titles.
4 Choose a horizontal or vertical axis title.
5 Enter the text for the axis title.

Legends

You can control the position of a legend relative to its corresponding chart. For example, you can place a legend on the left, right, top, or bottom side of the chart. To change the position of a legend, select the chart and click the Layout tab. Then, in the Labels group, click Legend and select an option.

Do it!

B-2:   Modifying chart elements

The chart is formatted as a 3-D Clustered Column.

If students applied a different chart type in the previous activity, references to "column" in this activity might not apply.

Here's how	Here's why
1 Click the **Format** tab	(Under Chart Tools.) You'll format some of the elements of this chart.
In the Current Selection group, click the arrow next to Chart Area	To display a list of chart elements.
Select **Series "Kendra James"**	To select only the data series for Kendra James.
2 In the Shape Styles group, click **Shape Fill**	To open the Shape Fill gallery.
3 Click the orange color swatch in the top row	To change the color for Kendra James's data series.
4 Right-click any one of the data points for Kendra James	(Right-click any orange column.) To display a shortcut menu.
Choose **Add Data Labels**	To display the value of the data point at the top of each column.
5 Click the **Layout** tab	You'll label the vertical axis.
In the Labels group, click **Axis Titles**	
Choose **Primary Vertical Axis Title**, **Rotated Title**	To insert a rotated title along the vertical axis. The default label "Axis Title" appears.
6 Triple-click in the Axis Title box	To select the text.
Type **Bonus sales**	
Deselect the chart	To observe the result.
7 Click **Sheet2**	
Click the chart	To select it.
8 Click the **Layout** tab	(Under Chart Tools.) You'll hide, show, and then move the legend.
9 In the Labels group, click **Legend** and choose **None**	To hide the legend. This chart doesn't communicate data effectively without a legend.
10 Click **Legend** and choose **Show Legend at Left**	To move the legend to the left side of the pie chart.
11 Save and close the workbook	

Unit summary: Charts

Topic A   In this topic, you learned how to create **charts** based on data in a worksheet. You learned that you can create a chart on a **chart sheet** or embed a chart in a worksheet. You learned how to identify various **chart elements**, such as axes, data series, data points, and the legend, and you learned how to create and edit a pie chart.

Topic B   In this topic, you learned how to apply different **chart types** and **chart styles**. You learned that you can format individual chart elements and you learned how to change the position of a chart **legend**.

Independent practice activity

In this activity, you'll create a column chart, add labels, and change the chart style. Then you'll format individual chart elements and move the legend.

The files for this activity are in Student Data folder **Unit 7\Unit summary**.

1 Open Projections and save it as **My Projections**. This is a simplified projected-profits worksheet.

2 Create a two-dimensional column chart, based on the quarterly expense, revenue, and profit data. Do not include the totals data. Be sure to include the relevant text labels. (*Hint:* When creating the chart, choose the column type called Clustered Column.)

3 Add the chart title **Quarterly Profits**. Place the title above the chart. (*Hint:* Click the Layout tab.)

4 Add a rotated vertical axis title that reads **Projections**.

5 Change the chart style to Style 3. (*Hint:* Click the Design tab.)

6 Change the color of the Profit series to green. (*Hint:* Click the Format tab.)

7 Move the legend below the chart. (*Hint:* Click the Layout tab.)

8 Move the chart below the data.

9 Compare your chart to Exhibit 7-2.

10 Save and close the workbook.

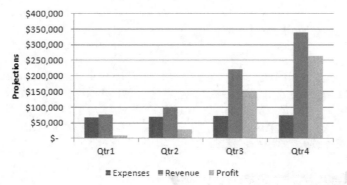

Exhibit 7-2: The completed chart

Review questions

1 What is a chart?

   A graphic representation of data.

2 True or false? If you update the data on which a chart is based, the change is reflected immediately in that chart.

   True

3 What is a chart sheet?

   A chart sheet is a separate sheet that contains only a chart, not the data from which the chart is drawn. You can move a chart from a worksheet to a chart sheet and back again as needed.

4 What is a legend?

   A legend identifies the data series in a chart.

5 True or false? A pie chart represents the total of all data points in a series.

   True

6 Describe two situations in which a pie chart is not the best option for charting a data series.

   - *When one or more values in the data series are zero or negative. These can't be represented visually in a pie chart.*

   - *When there are too many categories. This can result in overly small pie slices that don't communicate effectively.*

7 Describe a few ways that you can change or format a chart.

   - *You can change the chart type.*

   - *You can apply chart styles.*

   - *You can select individual data points and customize their formatting.*

   - *You can apply different chart layouts.*

   - *You can customize chart titles, axis labels, and legends.*

Unit 8

Managing large workbooks

Unit time: 60 minutes

Complete this unit, and you'll know how to:

A Freeze panes, split a worksheet, and hide and display data and window elements.

B Set print titles and page breaks.

C Navigate, manage, and print multiple worksheets.

Topic A: Viewing large worksheets

This topic covers the following Microsoft Office Specialist objectives for exam 77-882: Excel 2010.

#	Objective
3.4	**Hide or unhide rows and columns**
	3.4.1 Hide or unhide a column
	3.4.2 Hide or unhide a row
	3.4.3 Hide a series of columns
	3.4.4 Hide a series of rows
4.1	**Create and format worksheets**
	4.1.9 Hide worksheet tabs
	4.1.10 Unhide worksheet tabs
4.2	**Manipulate window views**
	4.2.1 Split window views
	4.2.2 Arrange window views
	4.2.3 Open a new window with contents from the current worksheet

Locking row and column headings in place

Explanation

On a large worksheet, only some of the data is visible at one time. When you scroll through the worksheet to see the rest of the data, the headings and titles move out of view, making it hard to interpret the data. You can solve this problem by using the Freeze Panes command. To make a large amount of data easier to work with, you can also hide rows, columns, and entire worksheets.

You can use the Freeze Panes command to "freeze" (lock) rows or columns in place so that headings remain visible as you scroll. To freeze rows and/or columns:

1   Select the area you want to freeze:
    - To freeze a row, click a cell in the row below it.
    - To freeze a column, click a cell in the column to its right.
    - To freeze both a row and a column, select a cell below and to the right of the row and column.
2   Click the View tab.
3   In the Window group, click Freeze Panes and then choose Freeze Panes.

To unfreeze panes, click Freeze Panes and then choose Unfreeze Panes.

Do it!

A-1:   Locking rows and columns

The files for this activity are in Student Data folder **Unit 8\Topic A**.

Here's how	Here's why
1 Open Product sales	You'll freeze panes to force titles and headings to remain visible when you scroll through the worksheet.
Save the workbook as **My Product sales**	
2 Scroll through the worksheet horizontally and vertically	As you scroll horizontally, the product names in column A move out of sight. When you scroll vertically, the headings in rows 4 and 5 move out of sight. To keep these names and headings in view, you can "freeze" them.
3 Select B6	You begin by selecting a cell below and to the right of the headings you want to freeze. By selecting B6, you'll freeze the headings in rows 1 through 5, as well as column A.
4 Click the **View** tab	
In the Window group, click **Freeze Panes** and choose **Freeze Panes**	To freeze panes above and to the left of the selected cell.
5 Scroll horizontally	To view the data in the other columns. The product names remain visible as you scroll horizontally.
6 Scroll vertically	To view the data in the other rows. The column headings remain visible as you scroll down.
7 Click **Freeze Panes** and choose **Unfreeze Panes**	(In the Window group.) To unfreeze the rows and columns.

Opening and arranging windows

Explanation

Objectives 4.2.2, 4.2.3

On the View tab, in the Windows group, click New Window to open a new window with content from the current workbook file. In the new window, the title bar displays the same workbook name followed by a colon (:) and the number 2, as shown in Exhibit 8-1. As you open additional windows, the windows will be numbered sequentially.

Because the new windows are simply a new view of the worksheet data and not a new file, any data changes you make are reflected in all of the workbook windows.

You can view all of the open windows at the same time. To arrange the windows:

1   Click the View tab.

2   In the Window group, click Arrange All to open the Arrange Windows dialog box.

3   Select the desired arrangement option and click OK.

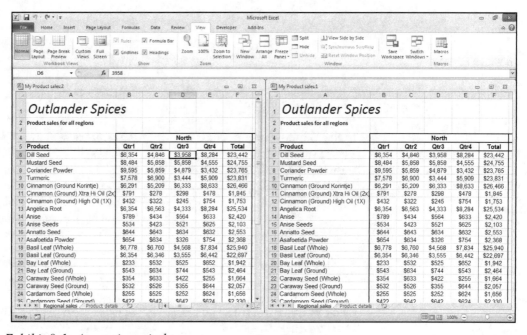

Exhibit 8-1: Arranging windows

Do it!

A-2: Opening and arranging new windows

Here's how	Here's why
1 Verify that the Excel window is maximized	
2 For the workbook, click [⊡]	To reduce the size of the My Product sales workbook window.
3 In the Window group, click **New Window**	To open a new window.
Observe the window title bar	[X] My Product sales:2 The workbook file name is appended with :2 to indicate that this is the second window.
4 In the Window group, click **Arrange All**	*Arrange Windows dialog box:* Arrange ⦿ Tiled ○ Horizontal ○ Vertical ○ Cascade ☐ Windows of active workbook [OK] [Cancel] To open the Arrange Windows dialog box.
Select **Vertical**	To arrange the two windows side by side.
Click **OK**	
5 Arrange the windows horizontally	Click Arrange All, select Horizontal, and click OK.
6 In either window, select D6	
Change the value to **4000**	The change is made in both windows simultaneously. This demonstrates that the two windows contain the same content and are in sync.
Undo the change	Press Ctrl+Z.
7 In the My Product sales:2 window, click [⊠]	To close the second workbook window.
In the My Product sales window, click [▫]	To maximize the workbook window.

Splitting a worksheet

Explanation

When using large worksheets, you might need to work with sets of data in distant locations on a sheet. By splitting a worksheet into panes, you can view different areas simultaneously. When you split a window, you can also navigate in each pane.

You can split a worksheet horizontally, vertically, or both.

Objective 4.2.1

- To split a worksheet horizontally, point to the *split box* at the top of the vertical scrollbar, as shown in Exhibit 8-2. The pointer changes to a split pointer shape, shown in Exhibit 8-3. Drag down to where you want to split the worksheet.

- To split a worksheet vertically, point to the split box to the right of the horizontal scrollbar, and drag to the left.

Exhibit 8-2: The split box at the top of the scrollbar

Exhibit 8-3: The split pointer

To remove a split pane, simply double-click the pane border, and the worksheet returns to a single pane.

Do it!

Objective 4.2.1

⚠ *The vertical split box will not be displayed if students did not unfreeze the panes in the previous activity.*

A-3:   Splitting a worksheet into panes

Here's how	Here's why
1 Point to the vertical split box	 (At the top of the vertical scrollbar.) The pointer changes to a split pointer shape.
2 Drag down to the line between rows 12 and 13	To split the window into two horizontal panes. Each pane has its own scrollbar.
3 Scroll down in the top pane	This pane scrolls independently of the other.
Scroll down in the bottom pane	This pane scrolls independently of the top pane.
In the bottom pane, scroll up	The headings and data in the top pane are duplicated.
4 In the top pane, edit B6 to read **$6,500**	Select the cell and type 6500.
5 In the bottom pane, locate B6	The value in B6 changed to $6,500 in the bottom pane also. The split panes are in sync.
6 Double-click the bar that separates the two panes	To return the worksheet to a single pane.
7 Point to the horizontal split box	 (In the bottom-right corner of the window.) The pointer changes to a split pointer shape.
Drag left to column F	To split the worksheet into two vertical panes.
Scroll in the left and right panes	To navigate in each pane.
Double-click the bar that separates the two panes	To return the worksheet to a single pane.
8 Save the workbook	

Hiding rows and columns

Explanation

You can hide individual rows and columns. This is useful when you want to focus on specific data or when you want to conceal formulas or other information.

To hide rows or columns:

Objectives 3.4.1, 3.4.2

1 Select a column heading or row heading, or drag across multiple column headings or row headings to make your selection.

2 Right-click the selection and choose Hide.

You can also select an individual cell or range and click the Home tab, click Format (in the Cells group), choose Hide & Unhide, and then choose an option.

Exhibit 8-4 shows a worksheet with only the Total columns: F, K, P, U, and Z. The columns in between—the columns containing quarterly sales details—are hidden so that the user can focus on specific data.

When you want to use or view hidden rows or columns again, you can unhide them:

1 Select the rows or columns on both sides of the hidden row(s) or column(s).

2 Click the Home tab.

3 In the Cells group, click Format and choose Hide & Unhide; then choose Unhide Rows or Unhide Columns.

Hiding and unhiding worksheets

Objectives 4.1.9, 4.1.10

You can also hide and unhide entire worksheets. Simply right-click a worksheet tab and choose Hide. To unhide a worksheet, right-click the active worksheet tab and choose Unhide. Select the name of the hidden tab you want to show, and click OK.

Point out the column letters, which jump from A to F to K, and so on.

	A	F	K	P	U	Z
1	**Outlander Spices**					
2	**Bonus sales for all regions**					
3						
4		North	South	East	Central	West
5	Product	Total	Total	Total	Total	Total
6	Dill Seed	$23,442	$20,345	$29,196	$35,902	$23,442
7	Mustard Seed	$24,755	$26,400	$34,879	$41,886	$24,755
8	Coriander Powder	$23,765	$29,688	$28,689	$36,485	$23,765
9	Turmeric	$23,831	$23,055	$37,545	$36,461	$23,831
10	Cinnamon (Ground Korintje)	$26,466	$33,404	$19,761	$41,993	$26,466
11	Cinnamon (Ground) Xtra Hi Oil (2x)	$1,845	$2,253	$2,139	$2,644	$1,845
12	Cinnamon (Ground) High Oil (1X)	$1,753	$2,146	$1,871	$2,819	$1,753

Exhibit 8-4: A sales worksheet with regional sales columns hidden

Do it!

Objectives 3.4.1, 3.4.3

A-4:   Hiding and unhiding columns and worksheets

Here's how	Here's why
1 Click the **Home** tab	If necessary.
2 Select columns B:E	(Drag across the column headings.) You'll hide detail columns so that only the totals are displayed.
Right-click the selection and choose **Hide**	To hide the quarterly sales details and display only the total sales for the North region.
3 Select columns G:J	You'll hide these columns by using another method.
In the Cells group, click **Format**	
Choose **Hide & Unhide**, **Hide Columns**	To hide the quarterly sales details and display only the total sales for the South region.
4 Hide the quarterly sales details for the remaining regions	(Select the columns you want to hide, right-click a selected column's heading, and choose Hide.) To display only the total sales columns for the five regions, as shown in Exhibit 8-4.
5 Select columns A:Z	You'll unhide the columns. To unhide columns B:Y, you must select the columns surrounding them.
6 Right-click the selection and choose **Unhide**	To unhide the columns. The worksheet displays the quarterly sales details for all regions again.
7 Display the **Product details** worksheet	(At the bottom of the worksheet, click Product details to switch to that worksheet.) You'll hide this worksheet.
8 Right-click the **Product details** sheet tab and choose **Hide**	To return to the Regional sales worksheet. The tab for the Product details sheet is no longer visible.
9 Right-click the **Regional sales** sheet tab and choose **Unhide...**	To open the Unhide dialog box. The Product details sheet is selected. It's the only worksheet currently hidden in this workbook.
Click **OK**	To close the dialog box, unhide the Product details sheet, and activate that sheet.
Return to the Regional sales sheet	

Objectives 4.1.9, 4.1.10

Minimizing the Ribbon to see more of the worksheet

Explanation

You can minimize the Ribbon to see more of the worksheet data. When you minimize the Ribbon, the tabs are still visible. Click a tab to use the options on it. When you're done using the tab options, the Ribbon is minimized again.

To minimize the Ribbon, right-click anywhere on it and choose Minimize the Ribbon. To show the Ribbon again, click any Ribbon tab and choose the option again.

Do it!

A-5: Minimizing the Ribbon

Students can also press Ctrl+F1 to minimize the Ribbon.

Here's how	Here's why
1 Right-click anywhere on the Ribbon	
Choose **Minimize the Ribbon**	The tabs are still visible.
2 Select B5:F5	
Click the **Home** tab	The Home tab options appear. You'll apply formatting to the range.
Apply the italic style to the selected range	After the option is applied, the Ribbon is minimized again.
3 Undo the formatting	Click the Undo button.
4 Right-click any of the tabs	
Choose **Minimize the Ribbon**	To disable this option and show the full Ribbon.
5 Save and close the workbook	

Topic B: Printing large worksheets

This topic covers the following Microsoft Office Specialist objectives for exam 77-882: Excel 2010.

#	Objective
1.2	**Print a worksheet or workbook**
	1.2.4 Apply printing options
	1.2.4.2 Print titles
3.3	**Create row and column titles**
	3.3.2 Print rows to repeat with titles
	3.3.3 Print columns to repeat with titles
	3.3.4 Configure titles to print only on odd or even pages
4.3	**Manipulate workbook views**
	4.3.3 Use Page Break workbook view

Print titles

Explanation

Before you print large worksheets, you'll typically want to set print titles and specify where page breaks should appear. Otherwise, your worksheet might print without important column and row headings on some pages.

If your data headings appear on only the first page, the data on the other pages will be hard to interpret. You can set print titles to specify which text should print as headings on all pages. To set print titles for a worksheet:

Objectives 1.2.4.2 , 3.3.2, 3.3.3

1   Click the Page Layout tab.

2   In the Page Setup group, click Print Titles. The Page Setup dialog box opens with the Sheet tab active.

3   Under Print titles, enter the range containing the titles that you want to print on each page. You can select the rows to repeat at the top of all pages, columns to repeat on the left side of all pages, or both.

4   Click OK.

Do it!

B-1: Setting print titles

The files for this activity are in Student Data folder **Unit 8\Topic B**.

Objectives 1.2.4.2 , 3.3.2,
3.3.3

Here's how	Here's why
1 Open Sales record	
Save the workbook as **My Sales record**	
⚠ *Students' PCs must have a printer driver installed for this activity.* 2 Click the **File** tab	You'll preview the Regional sales worksheet to see how it will look when printed.
Click **Print**	To display the print options and print preview.
3 Click through to page 4	◄ ⎹ 1 ⎸ of 4 ►
	(At the bottom of the window, click as shown.) This page doesn't show the product name row, so the data is difficult to interpret. You'll add print titles to all the pages to fix this problem for print output.
4 Click the **Page Layout** tab	
5 In the Page Setup group, click **Print Titles**	To open the Page Setup dialog box. The Sheet tab is active by default.
Objective 3.3.2 Under Print titles, in the "Rows to repeat at top" box, click 🔲	(The Collapse Dialog button.) The "Page Setup - Rows to repeat at top" dialog box appears.
Select rows 1 through 5	To designate these rows as print titles. A dashed line surrounds the selected rows.
6 Click 🔲	(In the "Page Setup - Rows to repeat at top" dialog box.) To maximize the dialog box.
Objective 3.3.3 7 In the "Columns to repeat at left" box, click 🔲	
Click the Column A heading	To set column A as a print title. Column A will now print on the left side of every page.
Click 🔲	To maximize the dialog box.

8	Click **Print Preview**	To display the results of the print titles. There are more pages in the worksheet because the Product column and the top headings are now included on all pages.
	Click through to page 6	To see that the data and regional titles above the Qtr columns change, but the top headings and product titles remain in place to provide context for the data on each page.
9	Save the workbook	Next, you'll apply page breaks to make the worksheet data print even more clearly.

Page breaks

Explanation

Excel inserts automatic page breaks that determine how worksheet data is divided among printed pages. Sometimes, sets of information that should appear together will fall on separate pages. To prevent this, you can insert manual page breaks.

To insert a vertical page break, select the column to the left of where you want to place the page break. (To insert a horizontal page break, select the row above where you want to insert the page break.) Then click the Page Layout tab. In the Page Setup group, click Breaks and choose Insert Page Break.

Page Break Preview

Objective 4.3.3

Page Break Preview shows you where page breaks are inserted when a worksheet is printed. You can drag page breaks to new positions to optimize your print output.

To preview page breaks, click the Page Break Preview button on the right side of the status bar. Manually inserted page breaks appear as solid blue lines. Automatically inserted page breaks appear as dashed blue lines, as shown in Exhibit 8-5.

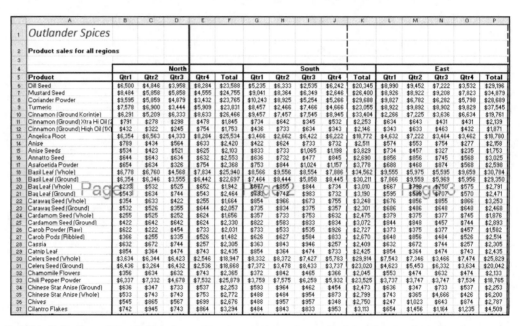

Exhibit 8-5: Page Break Preview, showing automatic and manual page breaks

Do it!

B-2: Adjusting page breaks

Objective 4.3.3

Here's how	Here's why
1 In the status bar, click ▥	(The Page Break Preview button.) You'll view the default page breaks and set manual page breaks that are better suited to this worksheet.
Select **Do not show this dialog again** and click **OK**	If necessary.
Observe the screen	A solid blue line between columns C and D indicates a manual page break. The dashed blue lines indicate automatic page breaks.

2 Point as shown

The pointer changes to a double-headed arrow, indicating that you can move the page break.

Drag the page break between columns D and E

This is still an incorrect placement, as it splits the North region's sales data unnecessarily.

3 Click the **Page Layout** tab

If necessary.

Select column E

Click **Breaks**

In the Page Setup group.

Choose **Remove Page Break**

To delete the manual page break.

Point out that faint page numbers appear in the background.

4 Deselect the column and observe the screen

The dashed blue lines indicate automatic page breaks. You'll set a manual page break after each year's Total column.

The page break's location depends on screen settings and printer drivers, so students might see it in a different spot.

5 Point to the first automatic-page-break line

The pointer changes to a double-headed arrow.

Drag to the right edge of column F

To move the page-break line, inserting a manual page break after column F. The page-break line is now a solid blue line. Now, only data for the North region will print on the first page.

Observe the next page break

The automatic page break that was between columns M and N has moved to the left. This occurred because when you move one page break, the other automatic page breaks shift automatically.

6 Move the second page break to enclose only the South region

Point to the page-break line between columns L and M and drag the page break between columns K and L.

Place a page break after each remaining region's Total column

7 Preview the worksheet

(Click the File tab and then click Print.) All of the data for the North region appears by itself on the first page.

Preview the other pages

Each region's data appears on its own page.

8 Save the workbook

Using different even and odd headers and footers

Explanation

Objective 3.3.4

You can print different headers and footers on even pages and odd pages. To insert different even and odd page headers:

1 On the Insert tab, in the Text group, click Header & Footer.

2 On the Header & Footer Tools | Design tab, check Different Odd & Even Pages. The header sections are now labeled as Even Page Header and Odd Page Header.

3 For the Even Page Header, insert text or a header element in the left section box.

4 For Odd Page Header, insert text or a header element in the right section box.

5 Click the File tab and click Print to view the new even and odd headers.

B-3:   Inserting different even and odd headers

Here's how	Here's why
1 Click the **Insert** tab	
In the Text group, click **Header & Footer**	Header & Footer
	The header and footer section boxes appear and the Header & Footer Tools | Design tab is active.
2 In the Options group, check **Different Odd & Even Pages**	☐ Different First Page ☑ Scale with Document ☑ Different Odd & Even Pages ☐ Align with Page Marg Options
	The header section label changes to Even Page Header.
3 Under the Even Page Header label, in the left section box, type **Page**	
Press (SPACEBAR)	
Click **Page Number**	(In the Header & Footer Elements group.) To insert an even-page header of "Page #."
4 Observe the Even Page Header	Even Page Header Page &[Page]
5 Scroll to display the Odd Page Header	
In the right section box, enter the same header text	Type Page and press Spacebar; then click the Page Number button in the Header & Footer Elements group.
6 Preview the worksheet	To see the new even and odd headers in Print Preview.
Save and close the workbook	

Topic C: Working with multiple worksheets

This topic covers the following Microsoft Office Specialist objectives for exam 77-882: Excel 2010.

#	Objective
1.2	**Print a worksheet or workbook**
	1.2.2 Print only selected worksheets
4.1	**Create and format worksheets**
	4.1.1 Insert worksheets
	4.1.1.1 Single
	4.1.1.2 Multiple
	4.1.2 Delete worksheets
	4.1.2.1 Single
	4.1.2.2 Multiple
	4.1.3 Reposition worksheets
	4.1.4 Copy worksheets
	4.1.5 Move worksheets
	4.1.6 Rename worksheets
	4.1.7 Group worksheets
	4.1.8 Apply color to worksheet tabs

Selecting worksheets

Explanation

Objective 1.2.2

An Excel workbook can contain multiple worksheets. You can easily move from one worksheet to another. You can also rename worksheets, change the color of the sheet tabs, insert, move, copy, and delete sheets, and print multiple sheets.

Tabs at the bottom of the window provide access to each worksheet, as shown in Exhibit 8-6. You can also press Ctrl+Page Down to move to the next sheet in a workbook, and press Ctrl+Page Up to move to the previous sheet.

If your workbook contains more than a few worksheets, Excel might not be able to display all of the sheet tabs at the same time. You can click the tab scrolling buttons to reveal hidden tabs.

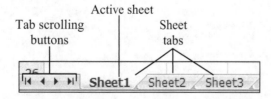

Exhibit 8-6: The tab scrolling buttons and sheet tabs

Do it!

C-1: Navigating between worksheets

The files for this activity are in Student Data folder **Unit 8\Topic C**.

Here's how	Here's why
1 Open Sales history	This workbook contains eight worksheets. Sheet1 is active and contains the bonus sales report for the North region for 2010. You'll use the sheet tabs to switch between worksheets.
Save the workbook as **My Sales history**	
2 Click the **Sheet2** tab	To view the data in the Sheet2 worksheet. It contains a 2010 bonus sales report for the South region.
3 Display Sheet3	(Click the Sheet3 tab.) To view the 2009 bonus sales report for the North region.
4 Switch to the Bonus sales report sheet	This worksheet contains the bonus sales report for the North and South regions for the years 2008–2010.
5 Click as shown	
	To fully display the Consolidate sheet tab. The Sheet1 tab is no longer visible (unless your screen is large enough to accommodate all of the tabs).
6 Click ⏮	To scroll all the way to the left to display the Sheet1 tab.

⚠ *If their screens are large enough to display the full Consolidate tab, have students reduce the size of the Excel window.*

Renaming worksheets

Explanation

By default, Excel names new worksheets consecutively as Sheet1, Sheet2, Sheet3, and so forth, but you can give them more meaningful names. There are three ways to rename a worksheet:

Objective 4.1.6

- Double-click the sheet tab, type a name, and press Enter.
- Right-click the sheet tab and choose Rename; then type a name and press Enter.
- Click the Home tab. In the Cells group, click Format and choose Rename Sheet; then type a name and press Enter.

Formatting worksheet tabs

You can color-code worksheet tabs so that it's easier to identify related sheets at a glance, as shown in Exhibit 8-7. Here's how:

Objective 4.1.8

1 Right-click a worksheet tab to display a shortcut menu.
2 Choose Tab Color to open a color palette.
3 Select the color you want to apply. Select another tab to see the results.

| North 2010 | South 2010 | North 2009 | South 2009 | North 2008 | South 2008 |

Exhibit 8-7: Sheet tabs can be color-coded

Grouping worksheet tabs

Objective 4.1.7

You can select multiple worksheet tabs by using the Shift+click method to select adjacent tabs. If you want to select non-adjacent tabs, use the Ctrl+click method. The selected tabs become a group that can be formatted or acted upon together.

With the grouped worksheets selected, right-click a worksheet tab and choose Ungroup Sheets to ungroup the sheets.

Do it!

C-2:   Naming worksheets and coloring tabs

Here's how	Here's why
Objective 4.1.6 1 Double-click **Sheet1**	To select the text "Sheet1."
Type **North 2010**	This name better identifies the sheet's contents.
Press ⏎ ENTER	
2 Rename Sheet2 as **South 2010**	Double-click the sheet tab, type the name, and press Enter.
3 Rename Sheet3 and Sheet4 as **North 2009** and **South 2009**, respectively	
4 Rename Sheet5 and Sheet6 as **North 2008** and **South 2008**, respectively	
Objective 4.1.8 5 Right-click **North 2010**	You might need to click a tab scrolling button to display the sheet tab.
Choose **Tab Color**	To display a color palette. You'll color-code tabs to clearly identify related sheets.
Select a green color swatch	
Click the **South 2010** sheet tab	To see the color of the North 2006 tab.
Objective 4.1.7 6 Select the **North 2009** tab	
Press CTRL and click the **North 2008** tab	To group the North tabs.
Apply the same green color to these two North tabs	(Right-click the sheet tab, choose Tab Color, and select the same color swatch.) Using the same color indicates that these tabs are related.
7 Group the three South tabs	Select the South 2010 tab, press Ctrl, and click the South 2009 and South 2008 tabs.
Make the South tabs blue	Select any shade of blue from the palette.
8 Save and close the workbook	

Managing multiple worksheets

Explanation

You can insert, move, copy, and delete worksheets within a workbook, just as you can insert, move, copy, or delete other items.

Inserting worksheets

You can insert a new worksheet by using any of the following methods:

Objective 4.1.1.1

- Click the Insert Worksheet button (to the right of the current tabs).
- Press Shift+F11.
- On the Home tab, in the Cells group, click the Insert button's arrow and choose Insert Sheet.
- Right-click a worksheet tab and choose Insert. Select Worksheet and click OK.

You can insert multiple worksheets at the same time by following these steps:

Objective 4.1.1.2

1 Use Shift+click to select the number of worksheet tabs that matches the number of sheets you want to insert.

2 On the Home tab, in the Cells group, click Insert and choose Insert Sheet.

Moving and copying worksheets

You can move or copy worksheets within a workbook, or to another workbook, by using the Move or Copy dialog box. You can also move a worksheet by dragging it to a new location. To copy a worksheet, press Ctrl and drag the sheet to a new location.

To use the Move or Copy dialog box:

Objectives 4.1.3–4.1.5

1 On the Home tab, in the Cells group, click Format and choose Move or Copy Sheet. The Move or Copy dialog box opens.

2 Select a new location for the worksheet from either the To book list or the Before sheet list.

3 If you want to copy the sheet (rather than move it), check "Create a copy."

4 Click OK.

Deleting worksheets

When you delete a worksheet that contains data, Excel prompts you to confirm the deletion because you cannot undo this action.

Objectives 4.1.2.1, 4.1.2.2

To delete multiple worksheets at the same time, you need to select them first. Click the first sheet tab, press Ctrl, and click the other sheet tabs. Then do either of the following:

- Right-click one of the sheet tabs and choose Delete.
- On the Home tab, in the Cells group, click the Delete button's arrow and choose Delete Sheet.

Do it!

C-3:   Working with multiple worksheets

The files for this activity are in Student Data folder **Unit 8\Topic C**.

Here's how	Here's why
1 Open Yearly sales	The Yearly sales workbook consists of seven worksheets. The North, South, East, and West worksheets contain regional sales reports. The other worksheets summarize data from the individual regions.
Save the workbook as **My Yearly sales**	
Objective 4.1.1.1 2 Click as shown	To insert a new worksheet. With this method, the new worksheet is inserted after all other worksheets.
3 Switch to the Report sheet	You'll insert a new worksheet before this worksheet.
On the Home tab, in the Cells group, click as shown	
Choose **Insert Sheet**	To insert a new worksheet before the Report worksheet.
Students will now use another method to insert a worksheet. 4 Right-click the **Report** sheet tab and choose **Insert...**	To open the Insert dialog box. The General tab is active and Worksheet is selected by default.
Click **OK**	To insert a worksheet before the Report sheet.
5 Double-click **Sheet1**	
Type **International** and press (↵ ENTER)	To rename the sheet.
Objective 4.1.3 6 In the Cells group, click **Format** and choose **Move or Copy Sheet...**	To open the Move or Copy dialog box.
From the Before sheet list, select **Consolidating data**	
Click **OK**	To move the International worksheet before the Consolidating data worksheet.

Tell students that they will now use another method to move a worksheet.

Objective 4.1.5

7 Point to the **Report** tab, and press and hold the mouse button

    You'll move this worksheet by dragging its tab.

  Drag the tab to the left of the Consolidating data tab

    To move the worksheet.

Tell students to click the tab scrolling button if the sheet tab is not visible.

Objective 4.1.2

8 Right-click the **Sheet2** tab

  Choose **Delete**

    To remove Sheet2 from the workbook.

9 Click the **Report** sheet

    You'll copy this sheet.

  In the Cells group, click **Format** and choose **Move or Copy Sheet...**

    To open the Move or Copy dialog box.

Objective 4.1.4

TIPS
  Students can also right-click the sheet tab and choose Move or Copy from the shortcut menu.

  Check **Create a copy** and click **OK**

    Excel copies the sheet, assigns it the name "Report (2)," and places it before the first sheet in the workbook.

10 Delete the original Report sheet

    A message box appears, warning that the sheet contains data.

  Click **Delete**

    To permanently delete the Report sheet. This action cannot be undone.

  Rename the Report (2) worksheet as **Report**

11 Save the workbook

Printing multiple worksheets

Explanation

Objective 1.2.1

You can print multiple worksheets at the same time. Hold down the Ctrl key and click the tabs to select the worksheets you want to print. Then click the File tab and click Print to display the print options and the preview window. Click Print to print the selected worksheets.

Do it!

Objective 1.2.1

C-4:   Previewing and printing multiple worksheets

Here's how	Here's why
1 Display the North sheet	You might need to click a tab scrolling button to display this sheet.
Press and hold ⟮CTRL⟯, and click the **South**, **East**, and **West** sheet tabs	To select a total of four sheets.
2 Click the **File** tab and click **Print**	To display the print options. The preview window shows that there are four pages. Each selected worksheet will print on a separate page.
Scroll through the pages	You could print these worksheets by clicking the Print tab at the top of the window.
3 Save and close the workbook	

Unit summary: Managing large workbooks

Topic A

In this topic, you learned how to **freeze panes** to keep selected row or column headings and groups of cells in place as you scroll through a worksheet. You also learned how to open a new window with contents from the current worksheet. Then you **split panes** to work in two worksheet sections simultaneously. Finally, you learned how to **hide** and **unhide** columns, rows, and worksheets to display only the data you need.

Topic B

In this topic, you learned how to set **print titles** so that headings appear on every page. Next, you learned how to set **page breaks**. You also used Page Break Preview to view and adjust page breaks. You created different even and odd **headers**.

Topic C

In this topic, you learned how to move between **multiple worksheets**, rename worksheets, and add color to their tabs. You also learned how to insert, copy, move, and delete worksheets, and how to preview and print multiple worksheets.

Independent practice activity

In this activity, you'll freeze panes, hide and unhide data, set print titles, and set page breaks. Then you'll insert, rename, and move worksheets.

The files for this activity are in Student Data folder **Unit 8\Unit summary**.

1 Open Inventory and save it as **My Inventory**.

2 Freeze the information in column A and rows 1–4. Scroll vertically and horizontally, and then unfreeze the information.

3 Hide these columns: Units purchased, Cost per unit, Units sold, Selling price per unit, and Units on hand.

4 Unhide all of the hidden columns.

5 If necessary, scroll vertically and horizontally to view all of the rows and columns.

6 Set print titles so that the company name, subtitle, product names, and region names appear on every page. (*Hint:* Make the first four rows and the first two columns appear on every printed page.)

7 Use Page Break Preview to adjust the page breaks so that the first page ends with the Total Purchase column.

8 Preview the worksheet to verify the results.

9 Change the name of Sheet2 to **Totals**.

10 Color the Totals sheet tab red.

11 Insert a new worksheet, name it **International**, and move it to the right of Totals.

12 Save and close the workbook.

Review questions

1 When you're working with a large worksheet, how can you lock row or column headings in place so that when you scroll, these headings will remain visible?

   Use the Freeze Panes command.

2 What is the difference between freezing panes and splitting windows?

   When you freeze panes, you can navigate in only one of the panes. The other pane is locked in place so that when you scroll, its contents (typically headings) will remain visible. In contrast, when you split a window, you can navigate in each pane.

3 True or false? You can split a worksheet either horizontally or vertically, but not both.

   False. You can split a worksheet horizontally, vertically, or both.

4 When you want to print a large worksheet, how can you ensure that your column and/or row headings are displayed on each page?

   Set print titles.

5 List three methods you can use to change a worksheet name.

   - *Double-click the sheet tab, type a name, and press Enter.*
   - *Right-click the sheet tab, choose Rename, type a name, and press Enter.*
   - *In the Cells group of the Home tab, click Format and choose Rename Sheet. Then type a name and press Enter.*

Unit 9

Graphics and screenshots

Unit time: 50 minutes

Complete this unit, and you'll know how to:

A Use graphics as conditional formatting to represent cell data.

B Insert and modify SmartArt graphics.

C Insert and modify screenshots.

Topic A: Conditional formatting with graphics

This topic covers the following Microsoft Office Specialist objectives for exam 77-882: Excel 2010.

#	Objective
8.3	**Apply conditional formatting**
	8.3.1 Apply conditional formatting to cells
	8.3.2 Use the Rule Manager to apply conditional formats
	8.3.4 Clear rules
	8.3.5 Use icon sets
	8.3.6 Use data bars

Data bars

Explanation

Objectives 8.3.1, 8.3.6

In addition to applying basic Excel formats such as fills and font colors, conditional formatting can help you represent data in graphical form based on defined values. You can create data bars and icon sets to depict values or divide them into categories. In addition, you can use data bars and icon sets to compare column values to one another. You can also use color scales to format cells differently depending on their values.

You can create the effect of a bar chart superimposed on a table of values by applying *data bars*. As shown in Exhibit 9-1, data bars show the values in cells relative to other cells in a range. A data bar's length represents the cell's value.

Sales per quarter						
Salesperson	Rating	Qtr1	Qtr2	Qtr3	Qtr4	Total sales
Bill MacArthur		$1,500	$1,750	$1,500	$2,700	$7,450
Jamie Morrison		$3,560	$3,000	$1,700	$2,000	$10,260
Maureen O'Connor		$4,500	$4,000	$3,500	$3,700	$15,700
Rebecca Austin		$3,250	$2,725	$3,000	$3,250	$12,225
Paul Anderson		$1,000	$1,700	$1,030	$1,000	$4,730
Cynthia Roberts		$1,500	$1,700	$1,800	$2,000	$7,000
Rita Greg		$4,590	$4,050	$4,500	$3,700	$16,840
Trevor Johnson		$3,660	$3,200	$3,000	$2,250	$12,110
Kevin Meyers		$1,790	$1,800	$2,000	$2,200	$7,790
Adam Long		$1,700	$1,950	$2,500	$2,750	$8,900
Kendra James		$1,650	$2,000	$1,500	$1,750	$6,900
Michael Lee		$2,050	$2,400	$2,600	$3,000	$10,050
Sandra Lawrence		$3,425	$3,750	$4,000	$3,120	$14,295
Mary Smith		$4,540	$2,700	$3,000	$3,200	$13,440
Annie Philips		$1,090	$1,500	$1,400	$1,000	$4,990

Exhibit 9-1: Data bars representing the values in a range

It's often helpful to widen the column in which you apply data bars. The bars' lengths are affected by the column width.

To create data bars:

1   Click the Home tab.

2   Select the range of cells in which you want to display data bars.

3   In the Styles group, click Conditional Formatting, choose Data Bars, and select an option.

Editing conditional formatting rules

Although the choices in the Conditional Formatting menu might serve your needs much of the time, you might want to fine-tune a few things, such as which cells are affected and what they look like. For example, by default, the smallest value in a range will display a very short bar, while the largest value will display the longest bar. Although this approach depicts the *spread* of values, it doesn't necessarily accurately represent the differences among them.

For example, if all of the values are between 900 and 1000, the differences in bar length will appear dramatically larger than they would with bars drawn on a scale of 0 to 1000. You can set parameters for the shortest and longest data bars based on numeric values, percentiles, percents, or even custom formulas.

To edit a conditional formatting rule after you've applied it:

Objective 8.3.2

1 From the Conditional Formatting menu, choose Manage Rules to open the Conditional Formatting Rules Manager dialog box, shown in Exhibit 9-2.

2 Double-click the rule you want to edit to open the Edit Formatting Rule dialog box.

3 Select settings as needed. For example, to make data bars more accurately reflect their proportions to one another, select Number from the Type list under Minimum, and then type 0 (zero) in the Value box.

4 Click OK to close the Editing Formatting Rule dialog box.

5 Click Apply to apply the revised conditional format.

6 Click OK to close the Condition Formatting Rules Manager.

Exhibit 9-2: The Conditional Formatting Rules Manager dialog box

Do it!

A-1:   Creating data bars

The files for this activity are in Student Data folder **Unit 9\Topic A**.

Objective 8.3.1

Here's how	Here's why
1 Open Quarterly sales	
2 Save the workbook as **My quarterly sales**	
Click the **Sales Per Quarter** sheet	(If necessary.) You'll create data bars to graphically depict the values in the Total sales column.
3 Select G5:G19	
4 Click the **Home** tab	If necessary.

Objective 8.3.6

5 In the Styles group, click **Conditional Formatting**	To display the Conditional Formatting menu.
6 Choose the first item in the Data Bars submenu, as shown	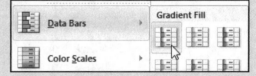
	To create blue gradient data bars in the selected cells.
Click outside the selected range	To deselect the range containing the data bars. The bars show up better when the cells are deselected.
Change the width of column G to **20**	To make the data bars longer. They now appear as shown in Exhibit 9-1.
	You'll change the data bars so they represent a range from the smallest to the largest value to more accurately represent the differences.

Objective 8.3.2

7 Display the Conditional Formatting menu and choose **Manage Rules…**	To open the Conditional Formatting Rules Manager. Because the default setting displays rules for only the current selection, no rules appear yet.
From the "Show formatting rules for" list, select **This Worksheet**	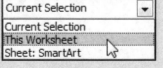
	To display the Data Bar rule you created.
Double-click **Data Bar**	To open the Edit Formatting Rule dialog box.

8	From the Type list under Minimum, select **Number**	Minimum Type: Number ▼ Value: 0
		To base the shortest bar's length on a fixed value.
	Under Maximum, change the Type to **Number**	From the Type list, select Number.
9	In the Value box under Minimum, enter **4000**	The lowest value in this column is 4,730.
	In the Value box under Maximum, enter **17000**	The highest value in the column is $16,840.
	Click **OK**	To close the Edit Formatting Rule dialog box.
10	Click **Apply**	To apply the revised rule. The bar for the smallest value ($4,730) is very short compared to the bar for the largest value ($16,840). There is greater contrast between the bar lengths.
		There are valid reasons to use different approaches (basing the minimum on zero or on a fixed value) for different purposes.
	Click **OK**	To close the Conditional Formatting Rules Manager.
11	Update the workbook	

Color scales

Explanation

Objective 8.3.1

Like data bars, color scales are used to format cells depending on their values. Color scales are applied based on a continuum of colors that correspond to the cell's values. This continuum can be based on shades of one color; for instance, the lowest values can be a dark green while the highest values show a light green. You can also show a transition between two or three colors, such as greens for lower values, yellows for middle values, and reds for higher values, as shown in Exhibit 9-3.

Clearing rules

Objective 8.3.4

To clear a rule and delete it from the Conditional Formatting Rules Manager, you can use either of the following methods:

- Select the cell or range containing the rule. Click Conditional Formatting and choose Clear Rules, Clear Rules from Selected Cells. (Or choose Clear Rules, Clear Rules from Entire Sheet to clear all rules.)
- Click Conditional Formatting and choose Manage Rules. From the "Show formatting rules for" list, select This Worksheet. Select the rule you want to clear and click Delete Rule.

	Sales per quarter					
Salesperson	Rating	Qtr1	Qtr2	Qtr3	Qtr4	Total sales
Bill MacArthur		$1,500	$1,750	$1,500	$2,700	$7,450
Jamie Morrison		$3,560	$3,000	$1,700	$2,000	$10,260
Maureen O'Connor		$4,500	$4,000	$3,500	$3,700	$15,700
Rebecca Austin		$3,250	$2,725	$3,000	$3,250	$12,225
Paul Anderson		$1,000	$1,700	$1,030	$1,000	$4,730
Cynthia Roberts		$1,500	$1,700	$1,800	$2,000	$7,000
Rita Greg		$4,590	$4,050	$4,500	$3,700	$16,840
Trevor Johnson		$3,660	$3,200	$3,000	$2,250	$12,110
Kevin Meyers		$1,790	$1,800	$2,000	$2,200	$7,790
Adam Long		$1,700	$1,950	$2,500	$2,750	$8,900
Kendra James		$1,650	$2,000	$1,500	$1,750	$6,900
Michael Lee		$2,050	$2,400	$2,600	$3,000	$10,050
Sandra Lawrence		$3,425	$3,750	$4,000	$3,120	$14,295
Mary Smith		$4,540	$2,700	$3,000	$3,200	$13,440
Annie Philips		$1,090	$1,500	$1,400	$1,000	$4,990

Exhibit 9-3: Cells under Qtr1 are conditionally formatted with color scales

Do it!

Objective 8.3.1

Objective 8.3.4

A-2: Using color scales

Here's how	Here's why
1 Select C5:C19	You'll conditionally format this range with color scales.
2 Display the Conditional Formatting menu	Click Conditional Formatting in the Styles group.
From the Color Scales submenu, choose the second option in the first row, as indicated	
Deselect the range	The cells are formatted from green to red, with shades of red representing the higher values, and yellow representing the middle values.
3 Update the workbook	
4 Select C5:C19	
From the Conditional Formatting menu, choose **Clear Rules**, **Clear Rules from Selected Cells**	To clear the color scale rule you just applied to this range.
5 Click	To undo the clear and restore the color scales in column C.
6 Update the workbook	

Icon sets

Explanation

Objectives 8.3.1, 8.3.5

You can also use conditional formatting to divide values graphically into groups. For example, you can assign stars to show ratings, arrows to show direction, or colored flags to indicate acceptance. Excel 2010 offers a variety of icon sets to meet your needs. To create this effect, apply *icon set* conditional formatting, as shown in Exhibit 9-4.

You apply and edit icon set formatting much as you would data bars. Here are some options you might consider:

- Display only the icons and not the values. You can paste-link the values into another column so the values appear in a separate column from the icons.

- Choose fixed values for the cutoffs for each icon. By default, icon set formatting assigns a value range of the same size to each icon. If each icon should represent a specific sales or rating goal, for example, you can specify that instead.

Sales per quarter						
Salesperson	Rating	Qtr1	Qtr2	Qtr3	Qtr4	Total sales
Bill MacArthur	☆	$1,500	$1,750	$1,500	$2,700	$7,450
Jamie Morrison	☆	$3,560	$3,000	$1,700	$2,000	$10,260
Maureen O'Connor	☆	$4,500	$4,000	$3,500	$3,700	$15,700
Rebecca Austin	☆	$3,250	$2,725	$3,000	$3,250	$12,225
Paul Anderson	☆	$1,000	$1,700	$1,030	$1,000	$4,730
Cynthia Roberts	☆	$1,500	$1,700	$1,800	$2,000	$7,000
Rita Greg	☆	$4,590	$4,050	$4,500	$3,700	$16,840
Trevor Johnson	☆	$3,660	$3,200	$3,000	$2,250	$12,110
Kevin Meyers	☆	$1,790	$1,800	$2,000	$2,200	$7,790
Adam Long	☆	$1,700	$1,950	$2,500	$2,750	$8,900
Kendra James	☆	$1,650	$2,000	$1,500	$1,750	$6,900
Michael Lee	☆	$2,050	$2,400	$2,600	$3,000	$10,050
Sandra Lawrence	☆	$3,425	$3,750	$4,000	$3,120	$14,295
Mary Smith	☆	$4,540	$2,700	$3,000	$3,200	$13,440
Annie Philips	☆	$1,090	$1,500	$1,400	$1,000	$4,990

Exhibit 9-4: The Rating column with icon sets applied, representing three ratings

Do it!

Objective 8.3.1

A-3:   Creating icon sets

Here's how	**Here's why**
1 Select B5	In column B, you'll create icon sets representing ratings for the salespeople based on their total sales. For you to do this, column B must contain the same values as the Total sales column.
2 Type **=**	To begin the formula.
Select G5 and press (↵ ENTER)	To complete the formula.
Copy the formula down the column	(Drag the AutoFill handle from B5 to B19.) Excel fills the result down the column, duplicating the values from the Total sales column.
3 Select B5:B19	If necessary.

Objective 8.3.5

From the Conditional Formatting menu, choose **Icon Sets**	To open the Icon Sets gallery.

Instead of widening the column, students will change the formatting to display only the icons and not the values.

In the Icon Sets gallery, under Ratings, select the indicated option	

An icon appears on the left side of each cell, along with the cell's value. However, the column isn't wide enough to display the values and the icons. Instead of widening the column, you'll change the formatting to display only the icons.

Objective 8.3.2

4 Open the Conditional Formatting Rules Manager	Click Conditional Formatting and choose Manage Rules.
Double-click **Icon Set**	To open the Edit Formatting Rule dialog box.
Under Edit the Rule Description, check **Show Icon Only**	

(In the bottom-right corner of the dialog box.) To hide the values in this column.

Next, you'll change the "breakpoints" (the threshold values) that determine which icon is displayed for a given value.

5 Under Type, select **Number** from both lists	To base each icon on a specific range of numeric values.

6	In the Value box to the right of the top icon, enter **10000**	(The solid yellow star.) To specify that only sales of $10,000 or greater receive this icon.
	In the Value box to the right of the second icon, enter **5000**	(The star that's half yellow.) To specify that only sales between $10,000 and $5,000 receive this icon.
	Observe the definition for the empty star	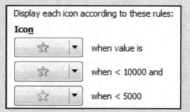
		Sales less than $5,000 will be assigned a star with no yellow color.
7	Click **OK**	To close the Edit Formatting Rule dialog box.
	Click **Apply**	To apply the revised rule.
	Click **OK**	To close the Conditional Formatting Rules Manager.
8	Center the icon column	The ratings appear as shown in Exhibit 9-4. The solid yellow star represents the highest values, and the outlined star represents the lowest values.
9	In D9, enter **7000**	Conditional formatting is dynamic. When Paul Anderson's total sales changes to exceed $10,000, the icon changes to a solid yellow star.
10	Update and close the workbook	

Before students change D9, have them observe the star.

Topic B: SmartArt graphics

This topic covers the following Microsoft Office Specialist objectives for exam 77-882: Excel 2010.

#	Objective
6.2	**Apply and manipulate illustrations**
	6.2.5 Modify Clip Art SmartArt
	6.2.6 Modify shapes

Inserting a SmartArt graphic

Explanation

A *SmartArt graphic* provides a visual representation of information. Excel 2010 provides many SmartArt graphic layouts that you can use to communicate your messages or ideas by combining shapes and text. After you've created an object, you can change its layout, content, and formatting.

To insert a SmartArt graphic, do this:

1   On the Insert tab, in the Illustrations group, click SmartArt.
2   As shown in Exhibit 9-5, SmartArt graphics are divided into categories depending on their purpose. In the category list, select the desired category.
3   In the List box, select the graphic that you want to create. A preview and a description of the selected graphic appear in the right pane.
4   Click OK.

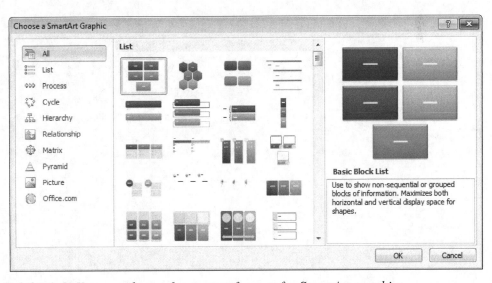

Exhibit 9-5: You can choose from many formats for SmartArt graphics

B-1: Inserting a SmartArt graphic

Here's how	Here's why
1 Create a new blank workbook	You will insert SmartArt in the new worksheet.
Save the workbook as **My Art**	In the current topic folder (Student Data folder Unit 9\Topic B).
2 On the Insert tab, in the Illustrations group, click **SmartArt**	To open the Choose a SmartArt Graphic dialog box.
3 In the left pane, select **Cycle**	
In the center pane, select the first format	
	(Basic Cycle.) A description appears in the right pane.
4 Click **OK**	The basic cycle diagram appears, with default colors and effects, on the worksheet.
5 Update the workbook	

Modifying SmartArt

Explanation

Objectives 6.2.5, 6.2.6

After inserting a SmartArt graphic, you can modify it by changing its layout, format, colors, text, and just about any other property. You can also apply 3-D effects, so objects can look tilted, contoured, or textured.

First, click the graphic to select it. Then, use the tools and Quick Style buttons on the SmartArt Tools | Design and Format tabs. *Quick Style* buttons apply several formatting properties at once, but you can also change all of these properties individually. You can customize the overall look of the graphic, the individual shapes, and the text.

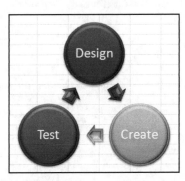

Exhibit 9-6: SmartArt with a Quick Style and Bevel effect applied

Do it!

Objectives 6.2.5, 6.2.6

B-2:   Modifying a SmartArt graphic

Here's how	Here's why
1 Select the SmartArt graphic	(If necessary.) You'll change some of its properties.
2 Click the **Design** tab	(Under SmartArt Tools.) There are many options here to format the graphic.
3 If you have room, drag the corners or edges of the SmartArt graphic frame outward	You can see the effects better if the shapes and text are bigger.
4 Click one of the shapes, but don't select the text	Click inside the shape but outside the [Text] area.
Press (DELETE)	To delete the shape.
5 Delete another shape	(Select any one and press Delete.) You should be left with three shapes.

6	In the top shape, click **[Text]**	To edit the text in the shape.
	Enter **Design**	
		You'll make a simple cycle diagram.
7	In the lower-right circle, enter **Create** as the text	Click [Text] and type "Create."
8	In the lower-left circle, enter **Test**	You now have a simple blue diagram.
	Deselect the shape	Click inside the graphic's frame but outside the shapes.

If time allows, let students experiment with different formatting options.

9	In the SmartArt Styles group, click **Change Colors** and choose the indicated Colorful option	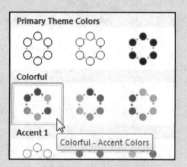
10	Click the **Format** tab	(Under SmartArt Tools.) The Shape Styles group offers both Quick Style buttons and tools for tweaking each item's properties individually. You will use Quick Styles to modify the shapes.
	Select the Design circle and its corresponding arrow	Click the Design circle, and then Shift+click the arrow to select both shapes.
	In the Shape Styles group, point to the Quick Styles and observe the SmartArt graphic	As you hover over a Quick Style, the SmartArt graphic reflects how the selected style would look.
11	Click the More button	To display additional shape styles.
	In the last row, select **Intense Effect – Red, Accent 2**	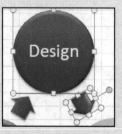
		To apply a Quick Style to the shapes. Multiple formatting changes have been applied with one click.

12 Use the Quick Style buttons to change the Test and Create circles and arrows	(Use Ctrl+click to select the shapes, and then click the desired Quick Style.) The Quick Styles that appear in the Shape Styles group now have an intensity similar to the recently applied Quick Style.
13 Press CTRL + A	To select all of the shapes in the SmartArt graphic.
14 Click the Shape Effects button	To display a categorized list of shape effects.
Choose **Bevel**	
	To display the bevel options. No bevel is currently applied to the graphic.
Select a bevel of your choice	(Any one will do.) Note that as you mouse over an effect, you can see a preview of it applied to your graphic.
Deselect the SmartArt graphic	Your graphic might now look something like Exhibit 9-6.
15 Update and close the workbook	

Topic C: Screenshots

This topic covers the following Microsoft Office Specialist objectives for exam 77-882: Excel 2010.

#	Objective
6.2	**Apply and manipulate illustrations**
	6.2.7 Modify screenshots
6.3	**Create and modify images by using the Image Editor**
	6.3.2 Use picture color tools
	6.3.3 Change artistic effects on an image

Inserting screenshots

Explanation

A new feature in Excel 2010 is the ability to insert screenshots into a worksheet. A *screenshot* is a picture showing what is on your computer screen. Because screenshots are static images, they enable you to "freeze" information before it changes. Also, screenshots can maintain the source formatting that might otherwise be lost if the captured information were copied and pasted into Excel.

To insert the entire window as a screenshot:

1 Verify that the window you want to capture is not minimized.

2 In Excel, click the Insert tab.

3 In the Illustrations group, click Screenshot.

4 From the Available Windows gallery, select the thumbnail of the window you want to capture as a screenshot. Only open windows are displayed in the gallery.

To insert a portion of a window as a screenshot:

1 Activate the window containing the content you want to capture.

2 In Excel, click the Insert tab.

3 In the Illustrations group, click Screenshot.

4 Choose Screen Clipping. The last activated window is displayed with a translucent layer over it.

5 Drag to select the area you want to capture. As you drag the mouse pointer, the selection becomes clear, as shown in Exhibit 9-7.

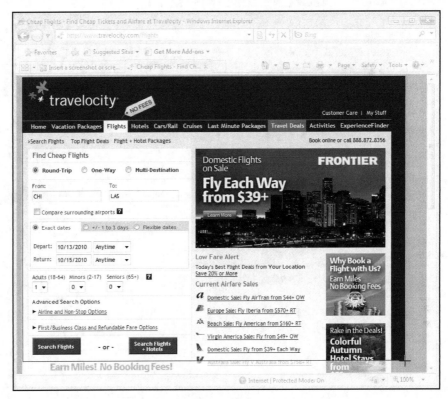

Exhibit 9-7: Clipping a screenshot

C-1: Inserting a screenshot

The files for this activity are in Student Data folder **Unit 9\Topic C**.

⚠ *Students will need an Internet connection to complete this activity. If no connection is available, have students capture the Windows Explorer screen.*

If students are asked to set up Internet Explorer, have them use the express settings.

Students can go to any Web site they prefer.

Point out that the Available Windows gallery on students' machines might be different from the graphic shown here.

Here's how	Here's why
1 Open Travel	
Save the workbook as **My Travel**	You will insert a screenshot from a Web page into this worksheet.
2 Start Internet Explorer	
3 Go to a travel Web site, such as Travelocity.com	The size of the window is not critical as long as it is not minimized.
4 In the taskbar, click the Excel icon	To switch to Excel.
5 Click the **Insert** tab	
Click **Screenshot**	
Observe the Available Windows gallery	
	The Available Windows gallery displays thumbnails of all open windows. Only open windows can be captured as screenshots.
6 Choose **Screen Clipping**	The Internet Explorer window appears with a translucent layer over it.
7 Drag to select a portion of the Web page	As you drag, the selected area becomes clear.
Release the mouse pointer	Your clipped screenshot is inserted into the worksheet.
8 Update the workbook	

Modifying screenshots

Explanation

After you insert a screenshot, the Picture Tools | Format tab appears. Screenshots are picture objects that can be formatted, moved, rotated, arranged, and sized like other objects in Excel.

Because screenshots are images, you can adjust the brightness and contrast, sharpen or soften the image, modify the color, and apply artistic effects such as Blur effect.

Objectives 6.2.7, 6.3.2, 6.3.3

To modify a screenshot, use the following galleries in the Adjust group on the Picture Tools | Format tab:

- Click Corrections and click the thumbnail to sharpen or soften the image or to adjust the brightness and contrast.

- Click Color and click the thumbnail to change the color saturation or color tone, or recolor the image.

- Click Artistic Effects and click the thumbnail to apply an effect to the image. For example, the Watercolor Sponge transforms the image so it resembles an Impressionist painting.

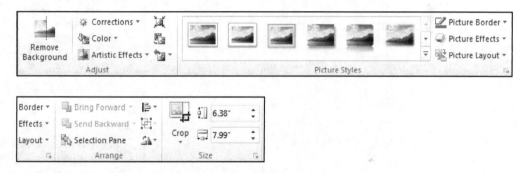

Exhibit 9-8: The Picture Tools | Format tab (shown in two parts)

Do it!

Objective 6.2.7

C-2: Modifying a screenshot

Here's how	Here's why
1 Select the screenshot	If necessary.
Drag the upper-left corner to F4	To move the screenshot.
2 Click the **Format** tab	Under Picture Tools.

Objectives 6.3.2, 6.3.3

3 In the Adjust group, click **Color**

To display the Color gallery.

Under Recolor, point to the **Sepia** thumbnail, as shown

The Live Preview displays the screenshot with the Sepia color applied.

4 Select a Recolor option of your choice	
5 In the Adjust group, click **Artistic Effects**	To display the Artistic Effects gallery.
Use Live Preview to explore the various effects	(Point to the gallery thumbnails to see a preview of the screenshot with the effects applied.) Many of the effects distort the Web page, so we won't apply any.
Click **Artistic Effects** again	To close the gallery without changing the screenshot.
6 Update and close the workbook	

Unit summary: Graphics and screenshots

Topic A

In this topic, you represented data graphically within cells by applying three forms of **conditional formatting**: data bars, color scales, and icon sets.

Topic B

In this topic, you inserted a **SmartArt** graphic. Then you modified that graphic by using the tools on the SmartArt Tools | Design and Format tabs, which include **Quick Styles** and other options.

Topic C

In this topic, you inserted a **screenshot**, and then you modified the picture by using the tools on the Picture Tools | Format tab.

Independent practice activity

In this activity, you'll create data bars and icon sets, and create and modify a SmartArt graphic.

The files for this activity are in Student Data folder **Unit 9\Unit summary**.

1   Open Fourth quarter. Save the workbook as **My fourth quarter**.

2   Click the 4th Quarter Sales sheet, if necessary.

3   Conditionally format the Qtr4 column with data bars of your choice. (*Hint:* Select C5:C19.)

4   Add the 5 Ratings icon set to the Rating column. (*Hint:* Set the column values equal to the Qtr4 values.) Show only the icons, as shown in Exhibit 9-9.

5   Update the workbook.

6   Click the Art Practice sheet.

7   Add a SmartArt graphic showing a hierarchy chart.

8   Fill in just a few names and positions of a fictitious company. Add and remove shapes as necessary. You can use Exhibit 9-10 for an example; however, your organization chart graphic will probably be different.

9   Format the chart with effects and colors of your choosing.

10 Update and close the workbook.

11 Close Excel.

Fourth-quarter sales		
Salesperson	**Rating**	**Qtr4**
Bill MacArthur	▂▃▄	$2,700
Jamie Morrison	▂▃▄	$2,000
Maureen O'Connor	▂▃▄	$3,700
Rebecca Austin	▂▃▄	$3,250
Paul Anderson	▂▃▄	$2,700
Cynthia Roberts	▂▃▄	$2,000
Rita Greg	▂▃▄	$3,700
Trevor Johnson	▂▃▄	$2,250
Kevin Meyers	▂▃▄	$2,200
Adam Long	▂▃▄	$2,750
Kendra James	▂▃▄	$1,750
Michael Lee	▂▃▄	$3,200
Sandra Lawrence	▂▃▄	$3,120
Mary Smith	▂▃▄	$3,200
Annie Philips	▂▃▄	$2,000

Exhibit 9-9: My fourth quarter workbook, showing data bars and an icon set

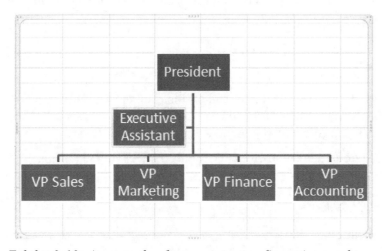

Exhibit 9-10: An example of an organization SmartArt graphic

Review questions

1 What's the difference between data bars and color scales?

   Data bars show bars in the cells. The length of the bars reflects the cells' values.

   Color scales shade the cells with a continuum of colors to represent the range of values in the cells.

2 How can you make data bars look more proportional to one another?

   In the Edit Formatting Rule dialog box, select Number from the Type list under Shortest Bar; then enter 0 in the Value box.

3 True or false? You can choose shades of only one or two colors for color scale formatting.

   False. You can use up to three colors in color scales.

4 What are Quick Styles in the context of SmartArt graphics?

   Quick Styles apply sets of properties, such as color and 3-D effects, so you can format graphics or text with one click.

5 Which object can be described as a capturing of the contents of an open window?

   A SmartArt graphic

   B Icon set

   c Screenshot

   D Clip art

Course summary

This summary contains information to help you bring the course to a successful conclusion. Using this information, you will be able to:

A Use the summary text to reinforce what students have learned in class.

B Direct students to the next courses in this series (if any), and to any other resources that might help students continue to learn about Excel 2010.

Topic A: Course summary

At the end of the class, use the following summary text to reinforce what students have learned. It is intended not as a script, but rather as a starting point.

Unit summaries

Unit 1

In this unit, students learned how to start Microsoft Excel and identify the components of the **Excel interface**. They learned **spreadsheet basics**, and they learned that workbooks consist of one or more worksheets that contain cells arranged in rows and columns. Students learned how to use the **Help** system to get information about Excel tools and techniques, and they learned how to open and **navigate** a worksheet.

Unit 2

In this unit, students learned how to enter and edit **text**, **values**, and **formulas**, and they examined the **order of operations**. Students also learned how to insert, move, and resize **images**. Students then learned how to **AutoFill** a series, **save** a file with a new name, and save a worksheet as a PDF file.

Unit 3

In this unit, students learned how to move and **copy data** in a worksheet, and use the Office Clipboard to copy and paste multiple items simultaneously. Then students learned how to move and **copy formulas** and use AutoFill to copy data to adjacent cells. Students learned about the limitations of **relative references** in certain circumstances and learned how to apply **absolute references**. Finally, students learned how to **insert** and **delete ranges**, rows, and columns.

Unit 4

In this unit, students learned that **functions** are predefined formulas that perform calculations. Students learned how to use the SUM function, **AutoSum**, and the AVERAGE, MIN, MAX, COUNT, and COUNTA functions.

Unit 5

In this unit, students applied **text formatting**, changed **column width** and row height, and aligned data in cells. Students also learned how to apply cell color, merge cells, and **format numbers** in several ways. Next, students learned how to apply **conditional formatting**, copy formatting by using the Format Painter and AutoFill, apply **table styles**, and sort data. Finally, they used Find and Replace to change cell formatting.

Unit 6

In this unit, students learned how to **check spelling** in a worksheet and preview a worksheet. They learned how to change page orientation, set margins, create and format **headers** and **footers**, and print gridlines. Finally, students learned how to **print** a worksheet and a selected range.

Unit 7

In this unit, students created **charts** based on data in a worksheet. They learned how to embed a chart, create a chart sheet, and work with **chart elements** (such as axes, data series, data points, and the legend). Students also created and edited a pie chart. They applied different **chart types** and chart styles, and changed the position of the legend.

Unit 8

In this unit, students learned how to **freeze panes**, split a worksheet into panes, and open a **new window** with contents from the current worksheet. They also learned how to **hide** and unhide columns, rows, and worksheets. Students then set **print titles** so that headings appear on every printed page, used different odd and even headers, and set page breaks. Next, students moved between worksheets and renamed and color-coded **worksheet tabs**. Finally, students learned how to insert, copy, move, and delete worksheets, and preview and print multiple worksheets.

Unit 9

In this unit, students represented data graphically within cells by applying three forms of **conditional formatting**: data bars, color scales, and icon sets. Students also inserted **SmartArt graphics** and modified them by using Quick Styles and other options. Finally, students inserted a **screenshot** of a Web page and modified it by adjusting the color and applying artistic effects.

Topic B: Continued learning after class

Point out to your students that it is impossible to learn Excel in a single day. To get the most out of this class, students should begin working with Excel to perform real tasks as soon as possible. We also offer resources for continued learning.

Next courses in this series

This is the first course in this series. The next courses in this series are:

- *Excel 2010: Intermediate*
  - Create 3-D formulas and links, and save workbooks as a workspace
  - Apply number formatting, merge and split cells, and add a watermark
  - Create outlines, summarize data, and create automatic subtotals
  - Create and edit named ranges, and apply 3-D names
  - Sort and filter list data, create tables and criteria ranges, and apply structured referencing
  - Save a worksheet as a Web page, create hyperlinks, and publish a worksheet
  - Format data points, create a combination chart, and apply trendlines and sparklines
  - Insert comments, protect a worksheet, share workbooks, and track changes
  - Change application settings and work with templates
  - Create PivotTables and PivotCharts
- *Excel 2010: Advanced*
  - Use the IF, OR, nested IF, IFERROR, SUMIF, and ROUND functions
  - Use PMT function, date and time functions, and array formulas
  - Use lookup functions and create data tables
  - Use the Data Validation feature and database functions
  - Export Excel data and import XML data from external databases
  - Use the Goal Seek and Solver utilities
  - Record, edit, and run macros

Other resources

For more information, visit www.axzopress.com.

Glossary

Absolute reference

A cell or range reference that does not change when a formula is copied; denoted by $ signs (as in cell B4).

Alignment

The placement of data within a cell.

Argument

The input value of a function.

AutoFormat

A predefined combination of text formatting, number formatting, borders, colors, and shading that you can apply in a single step.

AutoSum button

A tool that automatically generates a SUM function.

Cell

The intersection of a row and a column in a worksheet. Used to contain various kinds of data that you can format, sort, and analyze.

Cell styles

Predefined combinations of text formats, number formats, borders, colors, and shading that you can apply in a single step.

Chart

A pictorial representation of worksheet data.

Color scales

A type of conditional formatting that applies colors to cells, based on the cells' values.

Data bars

Bars that are displayed within cells to represent their values relative to other cells in a range.

Dragging

The action of pointing to a cell or an object, holding down the mouse button, moving the pointer to a new location, and then releasing the mouse button.

Embedded chart

A chart inside the worksheet on which it's based.

Function

A predefined formula that performs calculations ranging from simple to complex.

Icon set

A type of conditional formatting in which you use a group of icons to represent ranges of values.

Label

Text that identifies worksheet data.

Margin

The space between the edges of a page (worksheet) and its content. There are four of these: the top, bottom, left, and right margins.

Mixed reference

A cell or range address that has either an absolute column reference and relative row reference (as in $B4), or a relative column reference and absolute row reference (B$4).

Non-contiguous range

A selected group of cells located in different (non-adjacent) areas of the worksheet.

Operator

A symbol included in a formula to indicate the type of calculation to be performed, such as multiplication or subtraction.

Paste link

A link that enables pasted data to remain connected to its source. When the source data is changed, the data in the destination range automatically updates to reflect the changes.

PDF (Portable Document Format)

A file format that preserves formatting and enables file sharing. PDF provides a standard format for use by commercial printers. Adobe Reader is available as a free download.

Range

A selection that typically includes multiple consecutive cells.

Reference

A notation that identifies a cell or a range of cells in a worksheet.

Relative reference

A cell or range reference that is defined in relation to a formula's location. When you copy a formula containing relative references, they will change to reflect the formula's new location.

Screenshot

A static picture of the active window.

Shortcut menu

A menu of commands related to the object or screen element that you have right-clicked.

SmartArt graphics

Built-in objects that provide visual representations of worksheet data as well as add interest to a worksheet. SmartArt graphics can be formatted and modified like any other Microsoft Office objects.

Template

A special workbook that contains formatting, data, and tools to help you quickly create specific types of workbooks, such as invoices and expense reports.

Value

The raw data in a worksheet.

Workbook

An Excel file, which may contain multiple worksheets.

Worksheet

A document that consists of intersecting rows and columns which contain data.

Index